NORMALLY UNUSUAL

ISBN: 978-1-959457-20-6 (paperback)

Published in the United States by:
Blue Jay Ink, 451 A East Ojai Ave., Ojai, California 93023

Dedicated to...

FREEDOM

NORMALLY UNUSUAL

VINCE KITCHEN

CONTENTS

ACKNOWLEDGMENTS

"Writing is the deepest form of thinking."

So, in a way, thank you for "reading my thoughts." But, seriously,
thank you for spending the time that allowed me to share the depths
of my life and my "normally unusual" thoughts.

A tree makes no sound when it falls, if no one is around to hear.
Sound can only be heard.
As with writing, if no one is around to read it, it cannot be read.

So, thank you for reading my writing and
I'm thankful for the perseverance I found to have written
somewhat of a cautionary tale, loaded with a handful of hope.

Special thanks to all who donated to "Borders without Boards".
You put smiles on many children's faces in the Philippines.

On a much more personal level of gratitude, I would like to thank from
the whole of my heart my mother, Judy Kitchen, as without her, there would
be no me or this book. Along with my mother, I hold dear my first recollected
memory, a sunny day as we watched in wonder an insect living its life in the
grass off the sidewalk. Also, my father, Don Kitchen who is a generous and
stable provider of our family of five. He has been a great example of strength,
commitment and perseverance.

Without the help of many positive influences in my life, this book
could not have happened. My wife, Yolanda Guico Kitchen, who is beyond
a blessing (actually a miracle). Without her, I would never have had the time

to write. She is heaven on earth, an angel.

I would like to also thank Margaret Chamberlain. Her professionalism and guidance was a key factor in unlocking the editing of this book. She read my messy pen-printed pages and turned them into typed treasures of art work. Losing a liveaboard boat in a hurricane allow her to relate to my losing a home.

And, of course, to all with whom I share memories – you know who you are. A life is much bigger than a book can hold.

PRE RAMBLE
"THEN, HAPPENED, NOW"

Just out of high school, the knowledge didn't last. Didn't know where I was going, but I got there fast. Skatin' in the street, tired and beat. Living in my van, been like that for weeks. Skatin' down the street made me recall something my Dad said here, when I was small.

He said, "Follow your thoughts, I know that you can. Trust in me and make a plan. See it through and become a man . . . . boy, I hope you understand."

But, life was cruel and life was hard. I was never dealt that winning card. Ya see, I was bankrupt in my trailer park, as I heard my dog bark. Seemed like a long time since I rested . . . . seemed I kept gettin' arrested. Had a major operation, causin' great frustration. After that mission, out went the transmission. Then, of course, a divorce, caught the wife cheatin', couldn't take a chance of that repeatin'. So, I started drinkin', wasn't even thinkin'. Didn't mean to diss my one and only pancreas. Then, my dog died, and that's the first time that I cried.

See, now, some of my friends are liars, cheats and thieves. And what made you believe I was one of these. All I tasted in my mouth was misery and death. And, if you got real close, you could smell it on my breath. And, if I asked my God for some relief, do you think he'd return that whiteness to my teeth? Well, here I lived on the earth, so far from my birth. Here I lived wonderin' . . . . . just what was I worth.

There's more, back in '94, when the earth was shakin', my mobile home was taken. I was on the couch a yawning, when a tree fell and took out the awning. Then, in '98 things still weren't that great. Along comes a flood and took the yard with the mud. Seemed like my life was all full of crud. My Dad liked to call me Bud.

Anyway, I was hoping you could help me trudge through this obsession that will not budge, until I meet my judge. God, I hope he don't hold a grudge.

Sometimes when I'm talkin', it feels like I'm walkin'. Just a skippin' and a trippin' with people's ears. I be a flippin'. Maybe a lady or two be a drippin'. But, when I got home, I was all alone, just me, a dog and his bone. No one on the telephone, just an empty dial tone. Here in this lonely zone, I was on my own.

And, if you thought I was full of shit, you could of called me out of it. My number was 993-DIRT and my friends liked to call me Vert. That's short for Vertical, because I skate empty swimming pools and I cleaned the full ones as the "Water Wizard". Well, that's my spiel. I'm just here doin' the deal, tellin' you how I feel. And, when I'm outta here, I'll be spinnin' my wheels. Yes, I am REAL.

My name is Vince Kitchen and I used to be itchin' and twitchin', but now I'm feelin' kinda bitchin'. Some people don't like rap, think it's a bunch of crap coming from my trap, flippidy flap. I ain't here to tell you where it's at. We're all like the same cat. I just wear a different hat, that of a skate rat. This ain't no joke, on the pot smoke. I used to choke. I ain't like other folk - you can tell once I spoke. Kinda feels like I just awoke, but this time I didn't need to choke on a toke.

This ain't no jive, this is what kept me alive. My strive to survive is where I get my drive. You can take a dive in my pool, it's cool. You ain't no fool if you decide to change what's inside. You better take it in stride, because it don't always glide. But, if you got pride, you'll hang on for this ride. Good luck on the inside.

INTRODUCTION

To have a life come together and then fall apart.
And, now, to put the parts back together.

A memoir-like story of a Californian's countless action-packed adventures. As I enter into the second half of a century of life on this planet, I can see, upon self-reflection, that I have been living the life of a volunteer stuntman, Vince, since 1966.

To unlock the combination with alphabetical arrangements and to provide my communication with you will be a special challenge due to the fact I was diagnosed with dyslexia at a young age, combined with a quite obvious case of A.D.H.D.

After reading this collection of words about a "Normally Unusual" life that has experienced several natural disasters, including losing two houses. Also, including a life threatening drug addiction and a surgery that was blessed with the "anointing of the sick", also known as "the last rights", also, known as the sacrament "Kiss of Death", performed, by a priest, prior to the operation. This might lead you to believe my proclamation of self-diagnosed P.T.S.D. (Post Traumatic Stress Disorder). I can still remember all of my teachers by name, 1st through 8th grades at S.J.W. because of a strong memory, yet I can't remember which teacher said, "One day one of you may write a book." Never thought it would be me.

I may be underqualified to write a book, yet I accept this challenge that comes from the many people that know my story, that never seem to stop saying, "You should write a book" (Especially my Mom). Eleanor Roosevelt was quoted as saying, "You must do the thing you think you cannot do." So, here we go, look out below.

I may not be rich or famous, which always helps sell books. But, I am well-known and always getting by, knowing myself well. I can't afford to hire a ghost writer. So, I am the only hope I got to get this story to you.

I have noticed many of my lifelong friends are rich and famous. Just wait and you will see and maybe even agree with me when I claim to have a magnetic attraction to talented people.

This is undeniably true when it comes to the extreme sports arena. The athletes of whom I have ridden Moto-X, snowboarded, skateboarded and surfed with side by side have lead me down trails I would never had taken without them. It was a collective enthusiasm that gave birth to our extensive experiences.

I've been in magazines and newspapers, even a motion picture (extra in Point Break), on T.V. and radio programs, featured on the covers of dirt bike videos of the 90's. But, even with full page coverage, I still don't consider myself famous. That might come from the company I've kept, in comparison. I have had my 15 minutes of fame multiplied by 10 and still feel humbly unknown. Everything is perception and I have not always seen things clearly. With the internet and social media nowadays, it seems people have their 15 minutes of fame every day. And, through this social media (internet), some fans have contacted me over two decades later after seeing me on VHS video tapes. In these dirt bike videos, some of my personal quotes have made it from the mid-90's into the 2020's. "You're sending a boogie boarder out to do a surfer's job". This was a remark I made on film in response to the request that the film crew made for me to climb a huge cliff on my motorcycle, which I attempted three times unsuccessfully like a wipe-out artist! It makes me smile hearing people quote me three decades later.

I was born back in the day when we had to walk 8 feet through shag carpet just to change the channel on our black 'n' white television sets and adjust the rabbit ears.

I have resided in three countries, allowing me to flavor all types of behavior. Also resided seven collective years going mobile, living in moto-rhomes and travel trailers. A trippy, hippy gypsy, happy-go-lucky life style floating around this sea of land, staying surprised by not having a plan. Always looking forward to the unknown mysteries of what can only be known now.

CHAPTER 1

"CURB HOPPERS"

"Leaving anyplace, going nowhere, finding your now-here, the only agenda is to survive"

What I discovered, not in the pursuit of happiness, but rather in the happiness of pursuit. My perception is "Normally Unusual". Maybe my dyslexia has reversed my point of view. I view this as an altered consciousness, an enhanced view to a point.

As I see it, a skateboard has roughly 45 interchangeable parts. Numbers vary depending on microscopic analyzation. But, when the skateboard and skateboarder are flowing in motion, the equation is one.

They say, "You don't quit skateboarding because you get old, you get old because you quit skateboarding." Well, I am now undeniably old. Yet, I never stopped starting and probably wouldn't even if I could. It feels too good.

Just because you skate doesn't make you a skateboarder. Not being able to stop does. I found that to be true with alcohol also. You could call me a skate-o-holic. You could call me crazy, but that's always kept me from going insane. To remain sane and refrain brain strain was my largest gain. If you don't stay focused while skating, you will find pain.

Like Vans skateboard shoes, I've been around since 1966. By the early 70's I was on top of the world and a skateboard. Already the clay wheels had hit the scene, but my first experience on deck was a board with steel wheels. The effect produced from steel rolling on top of asphalt was a vibration of the whole body, centering in a tickling of the ears, pinpointing a buzz right between them. I was hooked.

My first impression was that the world was moving underneath me. Not the other way around. Also, kind of felt like a magic carpet ride. It was as mystifying as a genie in a bottle.

It was much later that same decade I would discover the mystery and misery in another kind of bottle. I found the taste to be as powerful as the genie's three wishes. And, my first wish was to have unlimited wishes. Then, later I wished I hadn't drunk past my limit.

In front of our house on Fullbright Avenue was the 1st sidewalk that lead to the 1st curb I would roll off and continue my magic carpet ride. Others in the neighborhood also found themselves here. Here, together, is where we formed our 1st skateboard club (brotherhood gang) "The Curb Hoppers". We had dues and weekly meetings. We were officially the 1st Sk8 crew I had ever heard of at the time. The sky was the limit and that seemed limitless.

My friends and I constructed a homemade skateboard of our own using one of my sister Lisa's steel wheel roller-skates, a piece of 2 x 4 wood and some nails. Yep, nails. It was like we were crucifying roller-skates so they could resurrect into a skateboard.

If you could bottle adrenaline, you would make a fortune. I have spent a fortune on the bottle and other drugs that are just an imitation of pure adrenaline. I actually paid for them twice. Once, when I got them, and once again when they got me.

As our tolerance grew, we searched for a bigger fix than hopping off the curb. So we built small ramps that could also be launched off with our Stingray bicycles with banana seats, sissy bars and ape hanger type handle bars.

I'm going to roll ahead to the mid 70's where it seemed like, what was our idea, had really caught on and in an explosive way in the form of skate parks. California's "SKATERCROSS" was the one that arrived right in the center of our vicinity - Reseda, the heart of the S.F.V. (San Fernando Valley). After school at S.J.W. (Saint Joseph the Worker), Chris Field and I would go there to experience the pleasure and the pain that was always awaiting us. After the bell rang, we would go to the restroom where all the jocks were changing into their uniforms. We would put on our skater gear. I remember appreciating not having to exchange my Catholic school uniform for another uniform. We had the freedom to choose which clothes we would soon rip and tear. And, at the skate park there always was a lot of ripping and tearing going on!

This was the 8th grade. In that changing room I also saw something that would later change my life. Someone was showing off that he had a bag of pot (marijuana). I had already gotten a talk about drugs from my police officer father. I remember him saying "drugs can permanently change your life." Well, that year I skated away on the thin ice of a new day actually graduating 8th grade without trying T.H.C. (tetra-hydro-cannabinol).

It was at S.J.W. grade school that I also saw my 1st "Surfer" magazine. Man, the pictures were so vivid it looked photo shopped, but I don't even think they had that type of technology back then. It did trigger a visual enhancement in my brain. I can still astro travel to the same tube rides of which I had photographically filed into my membranes. Today, when I see photos of my surfing, skating, snowboarding or moto-crossing, it is like an outer body experience. Now, looking back, a form of time travel. I had mentioned the name Chris Field? He would be one of a long line of best friends that would hit it big. The first magnetic pull toward talent in my life. My mom once said "You become your company." I didn't believe this at first. But, you will see as this story flows, what she said goes.

Skateboarding, playing guitars and B.S.A. (Boy Scouts of America) and later T.H.C. had brought Chris and I to some of the same trails to trip down. The love of music I still listen to today stems from the seeds he planted. He had it; I knew it. And, that one day, he would be world famous. If you Google him and link on X-Ray Dog, you will find he actually created a new genre of music. He was finally discovered and hired to make the soundtracks for

"Lord of the Rings" and several other blockbuster movies. Also, the theatrical trailers to movies, which really stir the emotions. The genre is called epic music. It is kind of gothic and very powerful. Chris can do anything. Check out his albums "Sub-Conscious" and "Beneath the Sun". For the 8th grade talent show he formed a band named "Allusions Now".

After S.J.W. we had to select a high school to continue our education. Chris and I ended up at St. Genevieve, which was a 30-minute bus ride each way. During these commutes is when I first tried pot.

I was thinking back to what my dad had said about "life changing". And, at the time, that sounded pretty good. I was looking at four more years of what I thought was total bullshit. For one, because at Catholic school back then they would swing at us with a weapon and swat us on the ass with paddles, plastic bats and sticks. Each teacher would have their own version of a torture device. And, I was getting my fair share of instigated torture. It would physically hurt for days and psychologically humiliate. I hadn't had a spanking since I was 6 years old for running away. Here's that (very short story version).

The L.A.P.D. patrolled the streets looking for me on my bicycle. As I peddled into a dark night, my dad was still in his police uniform when he applied my punishment for running away. It wasn't like police brutality, it was more like good parenting.

But, anyway I wanted a "life changing experience". I have not always heard everything I want to hear, but I have always heard things the way I want to hear them. The next 4 years were going to be tough and academically much harder than a public school. I had also at this time been diagnosed with dyslexia. This added to the difficulty.

So, my plan was to smoke pot for only 4 years, until this total bullshit was over. That was the plan anyway. Half way through the next year I was transferred to Chatsworth High (public school). Stoked, just where I wanted to be. At this place they had electives and no dress code. I took classes they didn't have at private school such as ceramics, print and photography. And, my senior year was beautiful. They would give you high school credits if you attended W.V.O.C. (West Valley Occupational Center). I took the cosmetology course there, thinking it would improve my chance of having girlfriends since the class was 95% females.

I already had an interest in cutting hair and girls. I had been sweeping it up for years. When I was about 13 my friend had a job sweeping hair, filling up shampoo bottles and making coffee for the cosmetologists working at a cool shop in the Northridge Mall called "Le Monico's" where they performed super styling new wave haircuts of the 80's in the 80's.

One day after skating we went to Burger King to get some free water. Well, my friend with the job, orders french fries. I wanted to buy some so bad. He said he couldn't buy me some, but let me have a couple. He also told me he would get me this job sweeping hair, so I could buy my own fries.

So it was on. I worked there for several years, starting at $2.90 an hour. That allowed me to buy more than french fries. I saw the people cutting the hair could actually buy cars and afford lots of pot. And, eventually I could get my fries through the "drive thru" stoned. And, that cosmetology class was a lot of fun! After 1600 hours of training and taking the State board examination twice, I finally got my license from the health department. So, by then I had a license to drive and another to cut hair. So, you were not safe on the street or in my chair!

At this time I was driving a 1972 V.W. Westfalia Pop-top camper van, sometimes driving through the drive thru in reverse just for the fun of it. Always getting strange stares as they would give me my french fries through the passenger side window. Now I see that may have been dyslexic behavior or possibly alcoholic behavior? You decide.

That van was like a fun size R.V. Motorhome, a sample of what would later be one of many different motorhomes and travel trailers I would be living out of. I spent a lot of time living life to the fullest out of that van. The tragic ending to that van's history would be the night I tipped it over and slid into the intersection where a police car was waiting for the light to change. My friend, Adam, was in the passenger seat with his arm out the window. It was a miracle he pulled it in just in time. It left a cool lightning bolt scar on his arm. I don't think his parents thought it was as cool as I thought it was. Though, I would have felt extra bad if he lost his arm because he is an extra good artist. My parents were having a party with their friends at our house a couple blocks away at the time. By chance, it was also the night my younger brother, Scott, had returned home after running away for 3 months. He was in the back of the van rolling around with the skateboards, surfboard, guitar and a 12 pack of beer and bong water splashing. He was thrashing while we were crashing.

Just before the accident we were skating down the hills behind our house when it began to rain lightly, just enough to make the streets slippery. So, when I saw the cop at the traffic light I slammed on the brakes, but I was going too fast, so I cranked the wheel sideways to keep from skidding into the intersection. Had there been no police presence, I would have just ran through the red light without a second thought, like so many times before. Fear always has its costs!! A whole book could be written solely on the adventures that van had. But, I will just keep rolling on.

Ok, so, I have to put it in reverse here and talk about dyslexia. It was about 9th grade when I was diagnosed with this learning disability. I was sent to therapy at a place called "Learning Skills". It was a strange rehabilitation program they had set up. Before massaging our foreheads and temples, they would have us jumping on a trampoline and recite the alphabet, each letter with each bounce, as well as visual exercises, switching an eye patch from one side to the other. This really didn't improve my grades, but it was peculiarly interesting. Turns out dyslexia is incurable, making this book extra difficult to write. It has also been written that alcoholism is incurable through medical attempts, but there is a spiritual remedy.

Many successful people have dyslexia as well. Well, I have heard it actually enhances other arenas within the brain. I perceive this "learning disability" with a normally unusual point of view, more of a view to a point. Neither making me more intelligent or less intelligent. I have always said, "I am twice as smart as you think I am, but only half as smart as I think I am". The norm is determined by the higher population percentage predicted by majority rules. The human eye of a so-called normal person has a reversal mirror image perception built in. Dyslexics may be carrying the missing link. I've always felt it was like my eyes were watching ping pong while I was attempting to read from left to right. There are some languages that read from right to left, but that was not going to un-dyslexic me either. The disorder is detectable in my spelling. And, so an extra big thank you to the person who did the proofreading for this book.

I used dyslexia as a reason to be transferred to public school, since I was failing the academically more difficult teaching of private school. It is hard for me not to get ahead of myself. I have always kind of been all over the place. I have a touch of A.D.H.D. (Attention Deficit Hyperactive Disorder) as well. Some can tell.

This was my opportune time to get away from the challenges and restrictions of private school. Not only because of the physical punishment, hard work and uniforms, but also to distance myself from the mentality of that rigid and strict authority. There was this one teacher that, if you got caught chewing gum in his class, you would have to put your gum in a jar of old pieces of gum from former offendees. Then, you would have to chew somebody else's A.B.C. (already been chewed) gum. I just couldn't accept, agree or relate to that mindset.

During this same time, I was discovering a whole new way of thinking. Dope. "Dopamine, an organic chemical of the catecholamine and phenylala-nine families that plays several important roles in the brain and body". Most likely where it got its name – Dope. Skateboarding also releases adrenaline which also releases dopamine. That merry-go-round ride soon turned into a roller-coaster, which I was willing to get in line to ride.

Simultaneously, I was discovering that alcohol was one of the "Top 5" most addictive drugs in the world. Pretty sure skateboarding made the "Top 5" in my world. Alcohol is to drugs, what rock is to roll. They go together as if they were one. The differences are only political. Making it legal does not make it any less addictive. If anything, more so. Growing up in the S.F.V. (San Fernando Valley) was pretty cool, and with a bus pass it was even cooler. This was a few years before turning 16 and getting a driver's license, which was the coolest. Well, back to the beach bus going to Santa Monica and Venice Beach with our boogie boards and bongloads. The sun and the sand, the sea and the land. From what I could understand, the whole world was at hand. But, what was unplanned, was the rope slipping from my hand.

One day we had taken the bus to the northwest corner of the Valley, to a place called "Stoners Den". We would enter down this crack in the earth, down a rope. We would squeeze between the rocks and boulders way down below the ground's surface to a small area the size of a bathroom. Lit up with lots of Bic lighters, where lots of kids and hippies would smoke a lot of pot – a lot. Then, we would exit on the other side of this small mountain. Very dark and claustrophobic was this place. Probably not accessible any more due to some major earthquakes, fire and flooding since then.

Anyway, near there was the Santa Susana Canyon. There a rope was tied to a tree. Being on the short side, I would have to really stretch out from the canyon wall while Chris threw the rope to me. I was under 5 foot tall at the time and could only reach it with one hand. The Tarzan plan was to jump and grab the rope with my other hand knowing I would need the strength of both arms to cross this canyon. After I jumped and reached out with my other hand, I missed the grab. After one arm took me as far as it could, the G-Force threw me into the oncoming canyon wall. This knocked me silly, dazed and confused for a few days. I remember it as a quantum moment in my life. One of the several times to come in life, I would be so lucky to still be alive. The feeling I had waiting for the bus after that experience was unforgettable. The wind was knocked out of me so hard it felt like I had survived nearly drowning, miles from the water. This left me thirsty for more.

The Chatsworth Hills were our playground. One time I fell out of a tree and got a concussion. This other time I climbed a tree with a six pack of beer, drank all six without even coming down to pee. Just let it flow to help the tree grow.

The train tunnels were carved into the side of the mountains of Chatsworth. To test our bravery, we would go inside the tunnel where there was a ledge of cement about 3 or 4 feet up on the sides where you could lay down while the train passed through. What made it scarier was that there was nothing to hang onto. The only thing keeping you from getting sucked into the vortex of this locomotive was your weight. Mine at the time was only about 90 lbs.

One time we saw a not so lucky dog who had gotten hit and cut into pieces by this train. From what I could tell it was a German shepherd.

Just a couple miles east of Chatsworth Hills was Brown's Canyon. That was the 1st place I tried L.S.D. (Lysergic acid diethylamide). I was 16 at the time. After heavy rains, that place would have a raging river. It was still raining when Chris Field and I took this raft (more like a swimming pool toy) way up the raging rapids. Catch was, there is a huge multi-level waterfall. We planned on getting out before that point. And, we did so, but we got out on the wrong side. So, instead of trying to cross the river which had grown in size, we decided to carry the raft across this downed telephone pole that stretched across this canyon about 25 feet above this waterfall. I went 1st holding onto the rope that was attached to the raft and Chris grabbed the rope on the other end. As we crossed over the roaring, muddy, growing flow of the freshly added rain water, things got a little shaky and my buddy let go of his end. This jilted my footing, so I released the rope from my hand as I recovered from a full tilt. As I finished crossing, I looked back, but saw no sight of Chris. Turns out he made it back to the wrong side again and was chasing after the raft. He had borrowed it from his little sister and really did not want to lose it. He caught up to it, but fell in the water when he reached for it. This took him floating and falling down the next few levels of this waterfall. There was so much force in the current that it actually ripped his shoes off and rocked his socks off. He lived, but I can't remember if we ever got his sister's raft back to her.

I have to mention, when we weren't thrill-seeking and defying death in the mountains around the S.F.V., we would hangout after the sun went down at "The Holiday Theater". My neighbor 2 or 3 years older than me, Bill, was the manager and caretaker of popcorn there. He also was my super good friend growing up, all the way back to playing Legos and seeing Pink Floyd's "The Wall" debut in 1979. So, he would hook us up and let us in for free. Stoked. It was a budget theater, kind of run down. Three movie matinees for 75 cents. I vividly remember seeing "Conan the Barbarian" and "The Blue Lagoon" there. Right next door was an arcade called "Pinball Alley". We would get fully tilted and play Asteroids, Defender and Pac-Man. It truly was an iconic place for the late 70's and early 80's. Mischief and mayhem and lots of rocker chicks in tight jeans, tube tops and a short skirt ready to flirt. Occasionally I would get hurt like an expert, which was always a great excuse to get drunk. Back then, I didn't need an excuse to drink, just the opportunity. And, that was my expertise.

We would tape string to a quarter and jig the pinball machines to give us so many free credits. It was here I learned how to make a mini time-bomb, by putting the fuse of a firecracker through the bottom of a lit cigarette. We would leave the theater and arcade after setting this up, let it burn and watch from the outside and laugh our asses off!

Speaking of assess being laughed off . . . . . this one time . . . . in B.S.A.

(Boy Scouts of America), we were coming back from a fishing trip in Mammoth Lakes. A bunch of us scouts were in the back of a camper that my dad and another scout's father were driving. The truck cab was separated from the camper, so we could get away with more mischief, undetected. We thought it would be funny to hang B.A's (bare asses), or more accurate B.B.S.A. (bare Boy Scout asses) through the back window at the cars traveling down the highway behind us. Well, the camper truck hit a pot hole in the road. This caused a scout to lose his balance and crack the window with his butt crack. It was pretty serious since his behind got all cut up and was bleeding. Not serious enough to stop us from laughing our asses off until our sides hurt. And, I'm pretty sure the travelers behind us were laughing their asses off as well. No butts about it.

"Normally Unusual Thoughts"
N.U.T.
(Another dimension to mention)
"Today was different, tomorrow will be the same"

And all this time I'm thinking I have the solution for World Peace. The whole time through grade school we were made vividly aware of wars. The school library had picture books loaded with photos of World War I and World War II. The Vietnam War was still in progress. These books terrified me with graphic pictures of dead bodies piled on top of each other from the Cambodian Genocide and Hitler's Holocaust. Arms and legs separated from men showing signs of insanity.

Also, we would have these safety drills where sirens would scream throughout the school speakers, followed by a change in our heart rate and breathing pattern as we would proceed to hide under our desks, just in case that day was going to be the day the Russians were going to blow us up. Even as a little kid, I thought I was smarter than the teacher – if she really thought my desk was going to save my life from the images I had just seen in the library.

Before school days had arrived and I was learning "good 'n bad" from Mom 'n Dad. I recollect asking them what was the worst thing a person could do? To this the answer was "to kill another person". This, of course, would get you a ticket to an eternity in hell. After all, it is the 6th of 10 commandments. "Thou shall not kill". I have always believed those ten were the only laws we ever needed. They would have been enough, but I guess politicians and lawmakers need jobs too. In the 1900's, we killed over 100 million of each other.

Anyhow, if life is short and eternity is unmeasurably longer, then wouldn't it be logically better to "be killed, than to kill". In a war-like situation or any major disagreement, our world for the most part, the majority, teaches us the opposite is true, "better to kill, than be killed".
The truth is, the majority is not right. "Majority Rules" – this point of view is fallible, because the majority lacks the faith to truly believe in an eternity. The fear of an end, is just a beginning of man's shortcomings. "Kill or be killed" is an inherent survival instinct learned through our collective consciousness. Fight or flight when our mind is not our own.

Seems to me if one had more faith than fear, that would determine the attraction of their action. Fear is a mind killer. Ultimately, if everyone felt this way, there would be World Peace. The survival conditioning of this collective consciousness has been installed into our D.N.A. But, still this is no excuse to kill and steal the life of another, no matter what your country's team captain tells you. No matter how much it helps our economy as well.

Changing our minds is the key; it's time to unlearn. To solve, we need to evolve from a caveman's survival mindset. We people have always manipulated words to suit our personal perceptions of reality. Some teams/ armies have even twisted it around making it seem that the ticket to an eternity of heaven would be granted to you for killing. My motto is "Believe and let Believe". We should all be allowed to have our own perception of reality. And, that would be possible if being killed for your beliefs was not an issue. We will need to extract the effect of fear with the impact of faith.

Are these thoughts "Normally Unusual"? I hope not. Faith, change and compassion are key answers to questions of "World Peace". To unlock this mindset could prevent a repetition of history. The answer is to question authority! I prefer to have questions I cannot answer than their answers that I cannot question.

If you have found contradictions in my theory, it was due to this - my mind is not my own all the time. Our culture, the time of which we are born and location of our upbringing, parental guidance and governmental ideology influence our thoughts. It's up to us to change our minds and unlearn the wrong that we cannot see until it is history. Life has to be lived forward, but is only understood backward. We are from the future, now. Written in stone, the best of the Ten Commandments is "Thou shalt not steal". It covers them all in theory. In all cases, one is taking something away from another. A life is not ours to steal. Faith and fear both demand that we believe in something that we cannot see. With this view, the choice is ours.

CHAPTER 2

"DESERT DAZE"

"God made DIRT, DIRT don't hurt"

On any Friday, our parents would pull Lisa and Scott Kitchen and myself out of school at lunch time. They would pull up to S.J.W. school in a camper loaded with pistols, rifles, shot guns and food, also towing a dune buggy and motorcycles behind it. Us three Kitchen Kids always felt so lucky and privileged to get out of school early. It was the icing on the cake of the finest dessert. Another trip to the desert. It was about an hour and a half drive to Black Butte and The Three Sisters. The whole way out to these desert daze, my Dad would be communicating with his buddies while we were caravanning out there with the C.B. radio "Desert Fox". He got the name from a tank general. In the Army, my Dad was in the tank division.

To help curb my anticipation, I would put my dirt biking boots on at the first site of a Joshua tree. After that it was just a countdown of cactus until we unloaded our steel horses and V.W. off-road rail dune buggy. Early before the sun rose, distinctively and indistinctively, from the flat horizon on the east, I had my boots back on, crackling and crunching with every step on the frozen dirt. In the desert, the nights would often get below freezing and the moisture from the dirt would rise to the top and form a crust that would coat the top of this part of the planet making it seem like another world. That was the icing on top of the desert, dessert-cake-textured dirt. A little more waiting was required before I could slice the dirt with my knobby tires. Simultaneously, waiting for the sun to thaw out the dirt and allowing my parents and others to awake without the sound of my motor being their alarm clock.

The Wileys, Ray 'n Louise, Kenny and Brenda were always there as well as many dirt biking friends of our family. My Godmother, my Mom's sister,

Linda Allen, Uncle Gary, our cousins, Damon 'n Shannon and my Uncle Billy also joined us on several camping weekends. Everyone would park their campers in a huge circle. From the top of the dormant volcanic mountain, Black Butte, it looked like the settlers of the old West on their great frontier. Their covered carriage wagons, a primitive prototype to our futuristic high tech campers.

The nights were loud with country western music, dancing and heavy drinking by the adults. Ignited with gasoline and a few tumbleweeds, we would blaze a huge fire in the middle of this circle. The fire being fueled by old tires. This was in the early 70's, before a great concern for our ozone was so widely apparent. Our supply for these tires seemed to be endless. There was an unattended dump a mile or so away, near an active turkey ranch. I'm guessing a tire shop dumped all their old used tires there. Anyway, we would stack the dune buggies with tires and even put a couple around our bodies and have a challenging ride on our dirt bikes back to the camp. After the steel belted type tires burnt, they would leave a mess of steel wire in the old camp fire spots from previous camping trips. I spent many a time cutting the wire out of my sprocket and chain after I would aimlessly ride through the ashes of these old fire pits. My small, but rugged 1975 XR 75cc Honda had a tool box integrated behind the front number plate. In there I also kept some tow rope for emergency. With urgency, I desired the need to pull down a Joshua tree with the rope and my motorcycle in a tug-o-war type fashion. As you might imagine, the Joshua tree was a lot older and stronger than the 10 year-old me and my 4-stroke engine. This defeat brought me face to face with the cake-textured dirt. This I found to be much harder and less tasty than I might have imagined. "Eat Dirt" was another of the many clichés my life would end up living up to.

Black Butte was our usual spot to camp and it gave us great shade from the hot desert sun in the evenings. The Three Sisters was another fun spot to camp, only being a couple miles from Black Butte. One weekend, half way through, we decided to switch camping spots. To save time and energy by not hooking the dune buggy back up to the camper, my Dad had my Mom drive the camper from Black Butte to Three Sisters separately. He must have thought she would drive it there slowly, since you can see both mountain sites from each other. But, she must have thought he wanted her to follow directly behind him while he blasted from spot to spot in our dune buggy, built for blasting through the desert (a trail with large bumps) Whoop-de-doos!!! While trying to keep up with my Dad going as fast as our buggy in our camper, she recreated the effects of a 6.8 earthquake inside of the camper. Every dish in the Kitchen's kitchen cupboard was tossed. In the camper, my sister and mom are in a full desert race with our dad in our buggy, while my brother and I are trying to keep up behind them on our motorcycles. This is a vision I will never forget. It's like there is this animated picture in my brain that pops up every once in a while.

Some nights before burning tires, us kids would roll them up to the base of the mountain, get inside of them and roll down the slope. I really enjoyed the dizziness effect that produced. Occasionally, we would find an old tractor tire which would provide enough space for more than one passenger - far from the type of carpooling we did earlier that Friday morning on our way to school.

With all that country western music, ropes, guns and the steel horses, we call motorcycles, it really created a cowboy kind of feelin', an aura we felt from one another. That "do it, in the dirt" vibe!

Coyotes always howled in the night. If one made its way into the turkey ranch, we were definitely made aware of it by hundreds of turkey gobbles gobbling up the cold night air. Sometimes we and the coyotes would surprise one another, when we would roll up one to one, eye to eye. And, yes, there was the occasional road runner, but his was no "Wiley Coyote" cartoon, although this sure was colorful. Hitting desert tortoises at high speed were equal to rocks that moved. We moved one to the S.F.V. to live with us as a pet, but he ran away.

Our family and friends would climb on top of the dune buggies with our rifles and drive really slow, at idle speeds, while looking for jack rabbits to scare up for target practice. That was fun, but I found it more exciting to find them when it was just me and my motorcycle looking for a hot pursuit. This would really tune up your turning and cornering skills. I'm still having flashbacks of some seriously fast jack rabbits and road runners, hopping and flying across the desert in front of me, always craving the lust for that kind of dust.

I cannot forget to mention the night rides in the buggies. They were so fun, but so much more fun if you were the ones in front, because the buggies following the leader always had to fight their way through the vision of walls of dust. Full moons were luminously helpful.

In this part of the Mojave Desert, there are a few abandoned houses that were built by western settlers and cowboys over a hundred years ago. Time turned these American dreams into great target practice for our shotguns. I preferred this to killing rabbits of which we hardly were ever accurate enough to execute. But, we sure did love the chase. For the most part, we just shot cans and bottles. My Dad is a great shooter. He once shot a quarter with a .38 caliber hand gun. I still have this memento almost 50 years after. The bullet actually bent the quarter and the slug is imbedded into it. Weird, because when he shot a quarter with the smaller gauge bullet through a .22 rifle, it would just leave a hole in the coin.

In 1972, under the Christmas tree, I found a 1969 Yamaha 60 cc motorcycle and this 6 year old was still wondering how it fit on Santa's sled, or at least how to explain how it fit to my younger sister and brother. Sitting on the bike, tippy toes stretched, I still couldn't touch the ground with both feet. At 9 years old I had received my first gun, a Winchester .22 caliber single shot rifle. My 4th grade fingers could not even reach the trigger. So, my Dad sawed off the butt of the rifle, allowing me to squeeze the trigger. This made me feel man-sized, being proportionate to my firearm. Showdown in the dirt, I was still just a little squirt.

As a young child my imagination allowed me to envision these mountains in another wise flat desert, as prehistorically dead dinosaurs. I pictured their fossils covered up by centuries of dust, as these large lumps and humps broke the horizon. One of these enormous dinosaurs or small mountains, depending on how you see it, was called "The Sand Hill." It was quite a distance from camp. We would travel there in our dune buggy and motorcycle packs, packed with ice chests full of beer and soda. Making it to the top of The Sand Hill was quite a challenge for both motorcycles and dune buggies. We actually have some footage of these triumphs on V.H.S. that were transferred from Super-8 film and later to D.V.D.

Sometimes we would crash on our effortful, yet unsuccessful attempts. This would allow sand to invade our clothes. This lead to rashes on our skin after the sweaty ride back to the camp. I often thought this dinosaur just thinks we are fleas on his back. But, afterwards, we would be the itchy ones.

Know risk, know reward. No risk, no regret. You can mix that saying up a bunch of different ways. What I'm saying here is that what we were doing was really fun, but also really dangerous. Through this view to a thrill, you can see reality bite your fantasy, real fast. And, sometimes reality bites. One of our riding buddies, Butchie, was riding at a new location that he and his Dad were not familiar with. Our family wasn't riding motorcycles that weekend. The five of us were probably at a lake waterskiing or something. It was 1979 and I remember my parents getting a phone call that kind of rang the beginning of the end to our desert daze, as a family.

Butchie had hit a rock that broke right through his helmet. This inflicted brain damage that altered his life, forever. The aftermath added up to the selling of their house to cover their medical bills. This brought great sadness to us, as he was a member of our motorcycle family. In the Kitchen household, the five of us cried as a family that night. As a family, our decade of dirt in the desert was drifting into another cliché, "every hello ends with a goodbye". There would be some more riding to be done as a family, but it was never really the same after that.

Pushing us to the end of that chapter, and of this, was this one lap around Black Butte. I was out on a solo patrol acting like Wiley Coyote chasing Road Runner. Anyhow, I rolled back into camp to see my dad's YZ125, my Uncle's CR250 and our friend's TT500 all missing. So, I asked my Mom, "Where did they go?" She said, "For a loop around Black Butte." This would be a two or three mile lap and I thought I couldn't catch up to them on my XR75. So, I said, "Which way did they go?" She pointed clockwise around the mountain. So, I figured the best way to find them would be to go counterclockwise and meet them somewhere on the other side of the mountain.

I'm going through the whoop-de-dos at a slight left hand curve, which limited my visibility. I was on the gas in 3rd, maybe 4th gear going pretty fast. Unknowingly, my Dad and his friends are racing down the same set of whoop-de-doos at a slight right hand curve, which limited their oncoming visibility. My Dad was in the lead. After eye contact, we only had one or two seconds before we hit head on. We almost missed each other, but my left front fork hit his foot peg. After my Dad hit the ground, my uncle hit my Dad. Uncle Gary rode over my Dad's legs. Luckily our friend on his big TT500 missed all three of us. As for me, I went flying over the handle bar and smack into the face of a whoop-de-doo, with my face. The impact of the sudden stop shattered my aviation goggles I was wearing for protection. These goggles were so old, they were made out of glass. Also knocked the wind out of me, counting the seconds to breathe again.

The connection of the two motorcycles hitting each other at that high of a speed caused my steel bike frame to crack in two. We later welded it back together, so I could live up to another cliché "get back on that horse and ride!" to overcome fear. I didn't want to become saddle shy. Sometimes falling feels like flying; it doesn't really hurt. But, it's that sudden stop that gets you.

Often on the way home from our adventures in the desert, we would stop by my Mom's parents' house and tell our grandparents about our delightful time in the dirt. I can still picture them shaking their heads in bewilderment. Then, there were the other times on our way home, we would stop by "MamaRita's Pizza". That taste and smell is still what I measure all other pizzas to. It was a low lit restaurant, candles on the tables, a lot of class. Relaxed enough for the parents to get good and drunk and dance to the jukebox. Well-stocked with country western music. This one song in particular, by Waylon Jennings, that goes, "She's a good-hearted woman loving a good timing man" – that fits my parents pretty well. No doubt in my mind that she was heaven sent. And, he was sent to show us how to have a good time!

It was a righteous way to end our weekends. This chapter of our lives was as good as family gets. It was those times I wish I could have frozen forever. But, as life goes, life goes on . . . . forever in memory.

"Normally Unusual Thoughts"
N.U.T.

"In the daze of my youth"

From here, now seeing things from a distance greater than a desert can provide, a lot has come into focus. As a process of zooming into my conclusions, trying to avoid illusions, I would ask my Dad and Mom a million questions when I was young. One question I clearly remember asking as my Dad was drinking beer and driving our motorhome. I said, "Dad, do you think you could have filled up a swimming pool full of beer with as much beer as you have drunk?" The answer was probably dependent upon the size of the pool. An average sized pool is about 25,000 gallons. I am familiar with this figure because I've spent almost 30 years cleaning swimming pools. If my calculations are correct, I have reached that quota. I used to drink like a fish. In those three decades of my career, I estimated I made over one million dollars cleaning swimming pools over 80,000 times. It isn't as much money as it sounds, considering I know I've spent more than that on over 30 motorcycles and 19 cars, a couple of houses and so many boards. Thank God for credit. I've had more than I deserved.

Another question I recall was, "Dad, this dirt biking is so much fun, why doesn't everybody do it?" He explained to me that not everyone can afford to buy dune buggies and motorcycles plus all the gas it takes to run them. You see, my Dad spent every minute that he wasn't being a thrill seeker working his ass off, and got paid good money. Not only was he a police officer, he also did side jobs for the movie studios as motor cop security. Plus, he had also gotten a real estate license and was selling houses to afford our fun times on the boat water skiing and in the desert kicking up dust.

Since then, I have lived in a couple different third world, poverty stricken, underdeveloped countries. It's very clear to see that there are less recreational activities going on in these places. The lakes don't have lines of boats waiting to get on for a day of relaxation; a completely different world.

I spent one year living in Costa Rica. Surfing is huge there. Surfing is a very low cost extreme sport, so it fits in well with some of these under privileged places, which happen to have really good surf. My best Costa Rican friend originally from Florida, Paul Minton, and I built a skateboard half pipe ramp under the roof of an outdoor restaurant. It was supercool and this one local kid would skate it with a large snake wrapped around his neck. His father would cook chicharrones only 10 feet from the action.

Now, as a result of marrying a beautiful, amazingly wonderful, and strong Filipino lady, of whom I deeply love, we are living here in the Philippines. We live in the capital of the Philippine Islands, which is Manila. Stuffed into a "manila envelope" comes to mind. Manila is one of the top 3 most heavily, densely, overpopulated cities on planet earth. With all this catastrophic over-population comes severe poverty levels. In the middle of all the chaos and confusion, the skaters I find here have skateboards with splinters and wheels more worn down than their tennis shoes and many don't even have shoes.

Over here I see things that make me sick, laugh and cry all in the same minute. It is so heavily congested that it is very overwhelming. Laced with anxiety like a bad acid trip. My mindset is not congruent with the average Filipino. I'm trying not to talk bad about the place. Shooting the messenger never helped the truth hurt any less. You don't have to look very far to see something you never thought you would, and hoped it wasn't true. Sad, but true. I won't repeat what came to view. I will keep it in my head until I'm dead. There is a lot of good over here at the same time too. Like most things, perception can flex. But, it can only bend so far.

There might be 10 times more people in Manila than Los Angeles, but it seems like there is 10 times less complaining, while actually having more to complain about – times ten. Sure, the cost of living is lower, but it is not relative. A pair of Vans shoes is twice the price in Manila. For example, gasoline costs are the same, but minimum wage is 90% less. Food and rent are cheap. Although it wouldn't be that difficult to spend a day's minimum wage at McDonald's in Manila. Extreme sports are way less common than one in a million here. They do not pay for labor by the hour. Their minimum wage is 512 pesos per day. That is about $10.00 US for 8 hours of labor. Likely including a 2-hour each way commute in the worst traffic known to mankind, on a smog-filled open air bus like vehicle they call "Jeepneys" (pronounced "chimneys") stuffed like sardines, in hot-as-hell conditions.

If you clean pools in California, you will make as much money in one hour as you would make in three days doing the same thing in Manila. Very controversial it is. This is a most uncomfortable subject to reflect. Inequality, humankind's biggest shame.

Often Filipinos ask me why I don't have children. I joke with my reply that "I'm still a virgin" and every time they laugh at that version. When I explain to people here that I never had any children of my own, they look at me with either pity or like I have not lived up to my obligation. The mindset here is to multiply. I was at church and heard the priest claim that "we are like trees, and if we do not bear fruit (reproduce) we should be cut down." Funny, because cutting down too many trees is a whole other arena in this circus of a self-destructive world. But, back to the point. The Pope came to the Philippines and even suggested they "quit multiplying like rabbits" to set things straight. Many people whom are childless get classified as selfish. I know I have been, in front of my back. I believe most accusations are self-reflective. We mirror each other. Normally Unusual as we think we are, reminding me of a quote from Albert Einstein, "Man's biggest illusion is that he thinks he is the only one". Other people's character defects are more visible to us than our own. Alcoholics Anonymous quote: "You spot it, you got it". Sorry about that, my mind started to wander.

I do agree that once you have a child your whole world is changed. Your plans now are not of yourself anymore. But, in the big picture and in the long run it might be equally selfish to have children, on a global level. Based on the theory that overpopulation causes poverty. From what I have seen, poverty causes pain and even death. Many poor people have several children as a hopeful pension plan, thinking when they are old their children will take care of them if each child pitches in a little. Poverty oppresses people to the point that even skateboarding, the least expensive of all extreme sports, becomes out of reach. Basketball is popular here, being one ball can accommodate many. Every 5 seconds someone is born and every 8 seconds someone dies. You do the math. I'm not saying I have all the answers to poverty and overpopulation. Though, it's not hard to see the connection. This leads me to believe it could be paramount to change the mindset of the collective consciousness. Please forgive me if this pisses you off. It's very upsetting and debatable all the way around. I'm not complaining about being in Southeast Asia where the culture couldn't be any further than the location itself from my home country and culture. My faith allows me to believe there is a reason I'm here. Teaching myself to learn. I feel like I'm caught between a rock and a soft spot. Sometimes it feels like a blessing and sometimes a punishment. Maybe, that just about sums up everybody's life everywhere. It's not normally unusual to have ups and downs within your highs and lows. And, that's just how it goes.

CHAPTER 3

"BOARD TO DEATH"

"Legends are born today as yesterday becomes tomorrow, turning them into unsung legends; songs forgotten."

I've read that a legend is someone who has altered the evolution of a selected lifestyle. Until then I had always felt a legend was someone of significance that you've heard of, but may never actually meet. Now, I believe that what you read influences what you feel. Changing beliefs gives way to a variable of truths.

The less fear you have, the more danger you can find. We have found that bravery and being legendary go hand in hand. I would like to give a hand to everyone that has given me a hand at handling the fear that came along with these dangerous circumstances we have navigated through together.

To all our friends that have died just trying to have some fun . . . . . . may we all "Board to Death".

Don Jayne earned the nickname "Drat", which stood for (Don) D. rat as in skate rat. Drat and I hung out a lot with days that began with surfing, and ended with skateboarding and beer drinking. Drat, being a few years older, could buy the alcohol. We would build skate ramps with wood that we would steal from construction sites in the night. Like rats stealing cheese. A rat trap caught me right in the face one night. In a hurry, not to get caught, Drat swung an 8 foot 2 x 4 around to load in the getaway vehicle. It hit my jaw so hard, I thought it was broken. No price is too high to pay for the adrenaline that wood could and would provide once attached to our ramp. Seems this life I've led came with a karma credit card, which I've never been able to pay off. But, the balance is much lower nowadays.

We formed a skateboard gang, crew, brotherhood or whatever you want to call it. We called it "Board to Death", on the premise that we enjoyed skating, surfing and later snowboarding so much we figured we would do it until we die. Draining and skating swimming pools was also part of our program, as well as seeking out really big full pipes. This mindset had us thinking in a full circle.

Drat and I were on an overnight tour in my V. W. camper van down at Upland Skate Park, also known as the "Pipe Line". Skating all day enjoying their huge full pipe. That was life enhancing to the fullest. During the night sleeping in the parking lot of the skate park, we were woken up to the sound of heavy pounding rain. The day began with the sight of 3 feet of rainwater sitting at the bottom of the pools. The clouds had cleared and this revealed white capped mountains.

Drat suggested we drive back to S.F.V. to pick up his snowboard and his dog, then get back on the road heading to Frazier Park's Mount Pinos. This was my introduction to skateboarding on the snow, or surfing on the snow. It's kind of like both meshed together and is highly addictive and was fairly unknown of at the time. The only option to get to the top of a slope was to hike. This was way before all the ski resorts would let us up on their chairlifts. We were pioneers of this new futuristic sideways sensation.

Drat is also an artist and airbrushed hats, t-shirts and such that he would sell at the swap meet. This was the incubation of the skate shop. Drat and I were assigned the green section (sector) of the color designated area to set up his stuff to sell outdoors. This might have planted a seed in my head to name it the "Green Sector" Skate Shop. The words were bobbling at the top of my head already. It came to solidify when on a road trip to Santa Barbara (Powell-Peralta) and Santa Cruz (Santa Cruz Skateboards) factories to buy skateboards. The words "Green Sector" floating around in my head while constantly having my mind on surfing a tube materialized. The 1st "Green Sector" skate shop located on Topanga Canyon was a success. Within a few years he moved it to a much larger location on Ventura Blvd., which turned out to be the largest snowboard outlet during that time period. I thank him for giving me the credit on inventing the title. Even 30 years later at my wedding reception, he included that acknowledgment during a toast.

"Green Zeen" would also evolve from this, leading me to believe I could make some money writing. Green Zeen was a magazine which I produced. Simply, I stapled Xerox copies of stories and action sport pictures of our ever growing Green Sector gang of friends, when I was bored to death. Seems I always have to have something going on. I would sell ad space in them for $100.00 per full page. Mostly, I used the barter system. For example, I traded "The Munch Box" a half page ad for 10 hamburgers. "Kennedy's Surf Shop" would always run a full page ad in exchange for surf gear. The price of the "zine" Green Zeen started publications at 44 cents and inflated up to 75 cents by the 7th issue. I made 500 copies of each issue. I still am hanging onto 4 complete sets of the volumes. Currently, they are considered to be archives of value to skate historians. Recently, I just bartered/traded a full set to Craig B. Snyder for a copy of his book, "A Secret History of the Ollie", which Barnes & Nobles listed at the price of $60.00. There is also a full seven-issue set of the Green Zeen on display in the museum at the Skateboarding Hall of Fame/ Skate U in Simi Valley, California.

Anyhow, back at Frazier Park, Mt. Pinos, my first slippery sensation snowboarding was done on an all wood Burton Snowboard sporting a big rubber strap across the back foot as a binding and for the front foot a water-ski-type binding. Strapped into these foot clamps I was wearing "Moon Boots" (super soft and too flexible). So, as I fell on my 1st attempt with some speed behind me, socks and feet slipped right out of these things. As the board and my boots continued the downhill run without me attached to them, Marina (Drat's dog) went chasing this ghost rider down the mountain. Little side note about this dog, Marina. If you threw a rock in the Jaynes' swimming pool, the dog would actually hold her breath, swim to the bottom and pick the rock up and return it to you. Kind of a rock bottom trick.

If I remember correctly, this snowboard was the same one that years later I bolted some skateboard trucks and wheels onto. I still have a picture of me street planting a curb at night behind Green Sector Skate Shop – on that creation.

By the early 1980's, most skate ramps, even quarter pipes, usually had a platform deck on top to prevent falling off over the back side. At my friend Tom's parents' house we had built a normally unusual platform deck, attachable to the top of my van. After school we would push this 7 foot quarter pipe out of the garage down the driveway and park my van behind it. Then we would secure a thick piece of 4' x 8' plywood to the roof of my van, sliding a mattress in between.

Well, one day we were in such a rush to get a rush from skateboarding, we didn't even wait to pull my van behind the ramp. Tom went to do a trick that required his hand to use the platform that was not there. His muscle memory had forgotten to remember, or not, and he fell right on his head to the asphalt street 7 ft. below. He proceeded to turn purplish-red in the head with his eyes rolled back. He started convulsing into spasmatic movements that made him look like he was being electrocuted. We were in shock. Tim, his little brother and Scott, my little brother and I didn't know what to do. Luckily, there was an unsung hero nearby – a gardener mowing a yard across the street. He came over and knew what to do. Like a savior, he miraculously performed mouth to mouth C.P.R. and got the skate rat breathing again. Receiving nothing from us but a "thank God you were here" comment, he went back across the street and finished mowing the grass.

Tom received a cast for a broken arm that day, which came in handy a few weeks later. We were at Chase Park one night just hanging out with our friend, Mike, Jayne (Drat's brother) and some girls, when some hot head came up and picked a fight with us. The freak head-butted me and knocked me down to the ground. Mike stood up for me and jumped in, but this guy was unstoppable. He wouldn't quit fighting. We piled into my van and took off, but this maniac was still hanging on to my van door now swinging at us through the passenger window. I'm already in 2nd gear and getting ready to shift into 3rd and Tom's smashing the guy's fingers with his cast, finally freeing us from this freaked out maniac.

This next sector (section) is a revised article from the "Green Zeen" I wrote well over 30 years ago.

"MEXICO"

South across the border is our destination, but equally excited we are about visiting the skate-world famous "Del Mar Skate Ranch", a little north of San Diego. The "Board to Death"/"Green Sector" brotherhood became so many on this trip, we needed two vehicles. Adam and Drat are following me and my van load of surf/skaters. The van was running on 3 out of 4 cylinders and a leaky head gasket which splattered the convoy with oil stains, peppering Adam's truck the whole trip. Literally, I would have to add a whole quart of oil with every tank of gas. We often had to push start it also, but it kept going and going and going.

So, we reach the skatepark, but it's shut down "Out of Business" with a big "No Trespassing" sign on the new chain-link fence. Of course, we jumped the fence and sessioned the concrete creation with the extra adrenaline you get while you're getting away with something. We took many photos of this session and the negatives of film are still in Mexico. I will explain that as it develops.

Next stop K-38's surf spot, because it's 38 kilometers past the U. S. border. The waves were perfectly clean and maybe some of the biggest surf we had ever been into at that point. This point break handles big surf well. Super glassy, sunny water just the right amount of cold and really just a great day to be alive. We were parked above the cliff at the point along with maybe 30 other vehicles all in a single row facing this wonder wave wonderland.

I remembered to smoke a few hits of pot on the top bunk of my pop-top van, but I didn't remember to put the pipe away in hiding. Meanwhile, I'm in the ocean about 60 feet below the van on the cliff looking up at my friends hanging around the open van as the policia are patrolling each vehicle with inspections. Then, I remember . . . . oh, no! I'm going to get my friends so busted. Luckily for us the policia must have found something in the car before ours. As they shook down our neighbors, I returned to the pipe and hid it well, then returned to the ocean with my friends.

After surfing until our arms and legs were noodles, it was fish tacos and cervesas till we passed out! Except for the anxiety of almost getting busted in a foreign land, it was for sure one of the top 100 days of my life. The true surfing lifestyle we were lucky to be exposed to. Speaking of exposure, back to the lost film.

After we had enough cervesa, pescado tacos and picture perfect waves, we headed back north to the "land of the free", "home of the brave". Driving in a foreign land gets confusing and I still don't think I made a moving violation. The policia said they spotted us speeding around a right hand turn. Crazy, because my top heavy camper van running on only 3 cylinders is almost incapable of speeding. As I'm getting hassled, Adam pulls up and parks behind the scene. Bill, who took most of the skate and surf photos gets out and starts taking pictures of the situation. The policia hombre called him over and says "let me see camera" in his best English. He grabbed the camera and ripped the film right out. After being exposed to the sun all day and now our film exposed as well, all that's left to frame our memories is our imagination.

As if that wasn't punishment enough, they then said "follow us back the station". So, we went from being pissed off to being way scared. Adam and I are following in our vehicles for a kilometer or two. This led us under a bridge in a kind of, sorta out of the way place, real private like. They step out of their patrol car with their hands on their guns, adding to our terror. It looked like they were going to draw their guns on us, but what they pulled out was a pen. El hombre actually drew on himself. He wrote the number "50" on his hand. That was going to be the cost of our freedom. Collectively between 6 of us we only had $44.00 and that was it. So, I guess we sort of got a deal, as they collected the ransom money.

As you can guess, we were broke, hungry and way hungover. The line crossing the border was time consuming sitting under very hot sun. Tom was feeling queasy and really wanted to throw up. He was kind of hung over the passenger door through the same window pane that he was smashing his cast over earlier in this chapter. He was patient, though, and didn't release the hostages from his stomach until we picked up some speed after crossing the border. Going the highway speed limit at last, he stuck his head out the window and splattered puke all over the side of my van. Over 3 hours later, we finally got home to S.F.V. where I could scrape off his crusty vomit.

V.W.V.
"Vertically Wild Vagrant"

All of it – well worth it. You can never pay too much for great waves with great friends and great memories. Grateful to be "Made in America". Sometimes you have to be in another country to see that we have it made in America!

Under developed countries with good surf have been well known to shake down surfers. This was my 1st time and I wish I could say my last. Twenty years later again in Mexico they got me for $100.00 with inflation and all. Also had to pay my way out of trouble 3 times in Costa Rica, but those tails are for another chapter.

Every perception has some distortion caused by some inherent perspective. Straight jackets and tax brackets. There is nothing funny about a funny farm, really. We are all assorted nuts trying not to crack. Skateboard madness is contagious, and this story outrageous. Close to the edge of going off the deep end.

It would be very difficult to live in this crazy world if you were sane. Enlightenment is unlearning the inherent thought that you were taught. All that is cosmic can also be comic. The opposite is true too, but only a few knew. What came first, the egg or the chicken? Personally I don't know if I became crazy from taking drugs or if I took drugs because I wasn't sane. Life is a succession of perpetual education. I remember Drat saying, "If anybody can understand and relate, I thought it would be you". I tried, and I will admit that I'm out there, but this stuff was on the other side of the o-zone.

Our trip to Santa Cruz was a turning point in Drat's life. The stop to Santa Barbara's Powell-Peralta skate factory to get supplies was like a kid visiting Willy Wonka's Chocolate Factory. But, by the time we traveled up to Santa Cruz to pick up more skate merchandise to sell at the swap meet, it was already midnight. Probably not a good time to eat the magic mushrooms I had brought along. But, we did.

I recall walking on the beach barefoot under the moonlight. Thousands of pre-existing footprints turned into faces all biting my toes as I stepped on their nose. I was so out of my mind at the time, I don't recall how the effects of the psychedelic hallucinogens influenced Drat's mind. He said he didn't feel a thing.

We missed a night's sleep, but the following day seemed to go normal. We toured the Santa Cruz Skateboard's warehouse and picked up more merchandise. The seller mentioned that we needed a business name to continue doing legitimate business there. So, floating off the top of my head, I threw out "Green Sector", which worked very well for the next 2 decades.

About a week or so later, things snapped. Later, leading Drat to wear his sunglasses at night. First sign things had changed in my friend was the vandalism of his own car. He spray painted the Rat Bones' trademark "Skate or Die" and "Board to Death" along with some obscenities to the establishment.

He contained more energy than a power plant. Near his house, the Winnetka Bowls (skate spot), there was a small full pipe we nicknamed the "Butthole". During the middle of one night, he took most all his stock of skateboards and hid them deep in the "Butthole". He thought they would be safer there. Well, his parents and society at large thought he would be safer in a different place. Tom, his brother Mike and I went to visit him there. This resort was without tennis rackets and outfitted its guests with straight jackets.

This was a very sobering site to see. Truthfully, I felt somewhat at fault for the condition his condition was in. I heard drugs can make you crazy, then they give you other drugs to make you sane. I thought the mushrooms had triggered the catastrophe. Turns out he was diagnosed with full blown bi-polarism. I don't know what goes on in there, but I do know that one day he escaped.

When he ended up back at Hotel California, the insane asylum kept him locked up there for three more months. After some time and many more nights wearing his sunglasses, Green Sector, would officially open the doors. Throughout the years in business he would sometimes need to leave town for vacations. He would leave me the keys to run the shop. I was honored and valued my time working there. He built a small quarter pipe behind the shop that was shreddable and tons of fun to skate.

Drat married a hot blonde named Teresa and they have two daughters, Kalie and Sara, whom both recently had children, making Don Jayne a grandpa. But, I still call him Drat.

Green Sector was very successful. That was very vivid when I visited him some years later at his one million dollar three-story house on the beach. But, being bi-polar means you're susceptible to getting back on that roller-coaster that has claimed many a life. Drat had another stay at (Hotel California) insane asylum after a divorce. But, that episode really sparked up a huge creative surge. He went on to produce short films and really got good at singing and playing guitar. Currently, he lives in front of a world class right-hand point break (Rincon) in a humble first floor of a beach house with some dogs and a great historic collection of skateboards. He surfs every day that the ocean offers him waves. Definitely a prominent figure in skateboarding. Board to Death.

"Normally Unusual Thoughts"
N.U.T.
"There is nothing spiritual about comparing . . . except here"

Coming from a spiritual being having a human experience, nothing is easy. For example, I found spiritual experiences in surfing, snowboarding, skateboarding, motocross and even writing. The better you get, the bigger the reward. The reward equivalent to the amount of satisfaction you receive from the experience. You get better from experience, from my experience. Life is a lot of fun, but (there is always a "but"). It's a lot of work. Even as I write this, there is some mental labor which will pay off as I'm reading. Self-discipline is required to endure the inevitable pain that is always spiced with pleasure, which is always included experiencing these activities.

Surfing, always my default thought of a parable for life. First, you have to paddle out and the bigger the surf, the harder that can be. Yet, normally the larger the surf is, the bigger the ecstasy payoff is. Skateboarding ramps can be pleasure spiced with pain. I've had a major hand in building 7 half pipes, all of which required acquiring the wood and many a hammer swinging to nail them together. Snowboarding used to require a lot of work hiking up the mountains. But, like the big trees in Paul Bunyan vs. The Chainsaw Story, chair lifts made them both congruently less difficult.

To me, the best line in a movie was "the only difference between us and the animals is the paperwork". What they were referring to in the movie "Planet of the Apes" was the red tape, the bureaucratic type. All the permits, certifications and loops you're supposed to jump through, all have a purpose I suppose, to clarify matters through clerical work. What's the matter with this I find is that everything changes, turning paperwork into clutter. They say we all have a paper trail. I find that hard to believe after being where I've been, knowing that a small part of the world's population today still lives in a primal and tribal state of existence. Many aristocrats may say these people are living like animals. Animals may be more efficient in some arenas. The civilized world needs jobs and clerical work provides a large percentage of the jobs our economy needs. Paperwork provides an un-natural order. I view over-organization as creating unnecessary frustration to the natural order.

No matter what you do, I'm proud of you. Simply because no one can do what you do exactly like you do what you do. As for me, I've cleaned swimming pools for 3 decades to finance my fun. So, no matter what we do, we all have to hike that hill, paddle out past the breakers and build that ramp, if you want to drop into that really fun stuff. Always in some way we have to pay to play. The pool pole was my cross to bear, skimming a million leaves, turning them into dollars.

What I want you to know is that you, probably unknowingly, will have an extremely powerful impact on someone's life. Whether you save someone's life or not, things you've done will affect others' lives generations from now. Whether you believe this or not, (in some small way or maybe in a huge way), this is undeniable. So, even at times when you feel helpless, know that you are being helpful. And, it helps ourselves to be helpful. This full circle effect I will talk about in future chapters as a road to recovery.

CHAPTER 4

"WATER WIZARD"

(Gravitation Experimentation)

"Time is money" is a paradoxical cliché. You can make more money, but normally it is in exchange for more of your time. So, you're constantly spending one way or another, simultaneously running out of both, hoping to buy more.

I had spent my required time at cosmetology school, an unreturnable 1,600 hours. Passed the State Board Health Department examination on the second try. I proceeded to the next level as a hair stylist, no longer sweeping up and washing heads of hair as an assistant. Paradoxically, I was actually making less money now. Business in the big leagues is a commission deal, so if you had a steady clientele, you could make some big bucks. The fact is that I wasn't cut out for cutting hair. Actually, I made an unsatisfied customer cry. I neglected to understand that her hair extensions were not going to react the same to the coloring agents as the rest of her hair did. This left her hair confused. Lots of chemistry and science involved. Another lady was equally distressed when I left the permanent wave solution in her hair so long that her curls resembled that of a frizzy poodle. Probably wasn't the best time to be smoking pot in my van while I left the solution in her hair. That stuff really warps time perception. Making what little money I deserved wasn't enough to make me show up at work on days that the local mountains had received fresh snowfall. The powder on the slopes was more of a calling than this hair career that was balding.

Still, I needed money. Many times a dollar short, but always a step ahead. I was 20 years old and wanted to move out of my parents' house. After I turned 18, they were charging me rent anyhow. Plus, all these skateboards, surfboards and snowboards of which I was constantly thrashing, didn't always come free. Not to mention, expensive lift tickets to Mountain High in Wrightwood.

Luckily, my skills on a snowboard got me noticed by an originator of the sport, Matt Donovan. Matt sponsored me on the spot and gave me a snowboard on our first acquaintance. Matt created a company named "Prop Snowboards". Prop Snowboards also covered the lift ticket expenses so I could ride the mountain as often as possible – and I did.

My financial stabilization came in the same form I found many skateboarding sessions, in swimming pools. This allowed me to start my own business as Water Wizards Pool Service. This opened the door to moving out of my parent's home. My new home would be a 27 foot camper trailer placed on 5 acres way up two long dirt roads in the mountains of Acton. You can take the surfer away from the ocean, but you can't take the motion away from the surfer. The pool route I was running at the time was in Palmdale, just 30 minutes from Mountain High. After cleaning 10 pools by early afternoon, I could get to blasting some airs on my snowboard several times a week. After a little more time and a little more money, I bought a used 1980 Yamaha 250cc four-stroke Moto-X motorcycle.

The man I was contracting 50 pools from allowed me to live and build a huge skateboard half pipe ramp on this 5 acres of land that he owned. After 6 months of swinging the hammers and buzzing the saws, my friends and I finished framing a skate structure 11-1/2 feet tall, 20 feet wide and 52 feet long. We had 30 sheets of 4' x 8' plywood covering the skateable surface. We had only 1 of 3 layers of wood already nailed and 60 more sheets sitting in a stack ready to apply when disaster struck. Call it bad karma or call it bad weather, but the wood we collected from construction sites at nights when rain would camouflage our illegal activity, got blown all over the neighborhood during a 100 mile per hour wind storm, leaving the halfpipe looking like a broken taco shell. We unfolded the project with a huge crane and finished the job. Small houses use less wood to build. Skating it was so fast and fun. The whole neighborhood enjoyed our creation, even if they did not skateboard. People would show up with tennis balls and rackets and play hillbilly racquetball. I recall my boss taking his quad motorcycle on it for some fun. It was huge and the largest out of 7 ramps that I have built in this lifetime. I realized I was living the skater's dream, even when awake, fully conscious. I had made friends with all the local Palmdale skaters. We were crazy wild and often jackassses. One of them made a profession out of it. England: Jackass "The Movie".

And now, into our 50's, over 30 years later, Dave and I ran into each other and resumed our friendship. We skated his half-pipe and shared some waves. And still communicate to this day. In fact, he shot the skateboarding photo used on the backcover of this book; which scored him an A+ in his high school photography class.

Growing up by the sea by means of a 20-minute drive to Malibu and now living the country lifestyle in the high desert, my valley surfer slang was now mutating to the vernacular of a "Billy" from the hills. You, as a reader, can give me any accent you'd like. That's one of the pleasures of reading. It provides an opportunity to decorate the stage, to set the lighting and sounds of the story that you translate from letters arranged for your decoding, if you will.

Acton was the perfect location for me, geographically in between the snow and the surf, with perfect dirt biking terrain right outside my front door. Maybe active dyslexia, or maybe not, but I noticed if I put an (i) in Acton, I (i) would be in the middle of the action. And, for now, I was at home in the middle of Acton.

In my 20's and 30's, I did so much driving, over 25,000 miles yearly, which is in the same neighborhood as the circumference of the world. Some mornings waking up, hours before first light to drive to the beach from Acton, surf, then drive to Palmdale to clean pools, and then occasionally to Mountain High after work for a night session, like an obsession. I had so much energy back in the day, I practically was levitating, like virtually on my board.

Matt Donovan (Prop Snowboards) lived in Summerland, a small beach town just below Santa Barbara. I would drive there and stay the entire weekends. Matt and I spent many hours in his factory (large shed) building snowboards, enthralled in really interesting deep and cosmic conversations.

Donovan's "Prop Snowboards" was actually the 1st twin tip snowboard, a game changer in the industry. There were never hard feelings whatsoever between the two friends, Matt and Chuck. But, Chuck's "Barfoot Snowboards" did get the notoriety for evolving the sport with the twin tip shape. Matt Donovan truly influenced Chuck Barfoot and Chuck was an inspiration to Matt.

Summerland's entire town is located on a steep hillside. This made it perfect for downhill sliding. This type of skateboarding was the closest flavor to snowless snowboarding at that stage of the game, cross/training. We had cut mitten-shaped plastic from the leftover materials we were making the snowboards from and glued them onto the palms of gardening gloves. These made great brake pads.

When slowing down seemed crucial to continuing life as we knew it, we would kick our boards sideways, laying out all kinds of karate looking stances perpendicular to the street. Sometimes the wheels would form flat spots from skidding sideways for too long, often times over 50 feet. Other times, we would launch our bodies forward in front of the board to create what we called the "Superman Slide". With this man-of-steel maneuver, flat spots on the wheels never occurred because your board was going in the same direction, straight down the hill congruently. The only time I would wear a helmet for this activity was when I wanted to perform a trick that I am pretty sure I invented. During this maneuver, I would actually drag my head down the hill, eyes just inches away from the speeding asphalt. The plastic skateboard helmet would slide alongside my sliding gloves. This trick I named the "head rush". This would slow me down, but still I maintained enough momentum to somehow pop myself up from horizontal to vertical again.

Matt Donovan is a man filled with enthusiasm. The word "enthusiasm" derives from a form of inner spiritual energy.

Snow is made up of 90% air. This allowed us to levitate carving over mountain tops, hovering over this layer of blessed snow, 10% water and 100% fun. Matt has this Christ-like aura surrounding him. Not only was his sponsorship to me a gift, his presence was a powerful guiding light in my early twenties. His little shack of a shop was a snowboard temple in my eyes. A palace of life to create these snowsliding devices and exchange stories of our lives. Him being a decade my elder giving me insight into the truer elements of its evolution.

When I entered the scene, it was the mid-80's and it was just starting to be accepted on the mountain ski resorts. Matt was old enough to experience the true evolution of the now Olympic sport.

Many of the characters from this era carried an artistic aura. You had to because none of this stuff had ever been done before. Creativity is clearly needed to focus on new visions.

In the company of Chuck Barfoot, Matt had a firsthand view to the trail on which Tom Sims and Chuck Barfoot parted paths. If you are curious to trip down that trail, please Google "The History of Snowboarding". Also visit "Scott Starr's Photography" – (@starrfilms) on Instagram. Scott's beautiful talent at documenting this era with angel-like angles is purely enjoyable. I was lucky enough to spend a day at Mountain High with Scott to have a photo shoot.

But, back to Matt, definitely one of the biggest role model/mentors in my life. Through his understanding of life, it helped me to understand that just because you have shared a great deal of time with a friend of a lifetime, you may not always be able to be in their presence for a lifetime. He once replayed the quote "ships drift in the night". The currents in life are strong and currently there is the entire Pacific Ocean between us. That has to be ok and it is, but in my mind we are closer, like heart to heart, soul brothers on distant shores.

The next super close friend close to the heart I would like to introduce you to is Don Szabo. When you see someone you have not seen in quite a while greets you with "Oh my God, you're still alive!", it makes you wonder if maybe not everyone has near death experiences as often as you, but Don and I have often heard that remark as we share this common bond. He has been close to the edge more times than you can count on your hands and toes. He knows life on the edge which he flows wherever he goes. If he were the one writing this book, it might sell more copies. This would be true due to the fact that he is truly world famous in the extreme sports arena of the 90's. I have probably shared more adrenaline-infused action sports with him than any other friend of mine. He is great at all of them, but likely most famous for snowboarding, making that his professional career for over a decade. If you Googled him, you could be entertained with hours of documentation.

I'm very grateful our ships have never drifted apart, figuratively. Just the other day he said, "We will be having adventures even when we are in our dentures". Which is great, because I have already started losing some of my teeth, and am wearing partials as I write. He was right.

Our meeting rooted in skateboarding. I had a half pipe in my parent's backyard. As a teenager, he heard about it, came over, skated and we have been great friends ever since. We share a multitude of memories skating, surfing, snowboarding, Moto-X, wakeboarding, jet skiing and thrill seeking adventures together. It is hard to pick which ones to share with you. Narrowing it down to a fraction of a percent here are a few.

Back in July, 1999, I cleaned a few pools in the morning, then met up with Szabo and Damon Huffman to go to the Mojave Desert, Red Rock. Damon is about as famous as they came in Supercross during that era, holding two championship 125cc Supercross titles. And, having held on to factory team sponsorships with Suzuki, Honda and Kawasaki in the mid-90's to mid 2,000's. More about that later. I'm trying to stay on the trail here.

It was hot, sweaty hot, in a monsoonal way, huge and high pressure clouds hovered above in the sky. Normally unusual for July when the desert is known for its dusty and dry terrain. Not the best traction for the desires of our tires. We were hoping the clouds would release rain to produce that chocolate cake type of dirt that all dirt bikers find appetizing. Loaded in Damon's truck with my '97 KX250, Szabo's '98 KX250 and Huffman's '99 KX250 factory ride in the back, the three green Kawasaki machines were ready to dice and slice through the desert on a fresh canvas of delicious dirt.

It rained like crazy for an hour, then stopped. We all had spent a lot of time riding in the desert, but I believe this was the first flash flood any of us had witnessed with an in-person view. It was amazing and surreal. The desert has many sand washes that are created over centuries due to these phenomenon. What happens is that more water is being delivered than the ground has time to saturate, causing temporary raging rivers that are very powerful, knocking and tearing down everything in their path. In the after-math of this brief, but potent storm, the desert was left picture perfect in the eyes of a dirt biker.

Damon always knew how to find these great tracks in places where many get lost. I cherish this memory I have of Szabo and me sitting up on a majestic hillside like two Indians on steel horses watching the magical artistry of our friend below carving fast and precise lines of accuracy down in this desert valley, leaving an impression of a mind painting.

This hidden away track was perfect for Damon to get some training in for the A.M.A. Nationals (the biggest race series in the United States) which he was in the midst of contending.

From there the three of us continued to draw lines painting the ancient, yet fresh desert, with our roosts up and down steep mountains, deep flowing sand washes and blasting up over vertical cliffs. Here, I was in the middle of my favorite world with two of the world's most talented human beings. Wanting to prove to myself and them that they were also in good company, I started to ride a little over my head showing off on this cliff climb we had found, finding myself out of control. Surprising to me, this cliff had no flat spot on top to land on. It just dropped off to an unseen ditch-like valley. In hindsight, I should have looked before I leaped. No regrets; after crashes I receive a revival of survival euphoria. Wiping-out can be even more exciting than pulling off a maneuver. Definitely a forced, fear facing part of action sports.

"When in doubt, gas it!" is sometimes good advice. And, in this situation quite helpful. A twist of the throttle I needed to do to get the bike far from me so I wouldn't become a flat spot for it to land on. As I ejected the bike, the spinning back tire hooked up with great traction and launched clear to the other side of this small valley crashing the front tire first into the other side with a dynamite impact. End result – I was peaking on adrenaline and my forks to my front wheel were so bent and twisted that they would not release compression, therefore leaving my bike in a stinkbug stance. I could still ride it back to the truck, but for me, all performance riding was done for the day.

A decade prior to flashing back to that flash flood, Szabo and I skated a half pipe in a demo to promote a bike/skate shop named "Bicycle Radness" in Palmdale, California. Mike McGill was skating with us. If you know skateboarding, you know of Mike McGill of the Bones Brigade and Powell Peralta, also the innovator skater of the McTwist (a 540⊠ spinning inverted aerial). The photos I have from that day are in black and white, adding to the nostalgia of it all. Always extremely fun to skate with Szabo and skating with McGill in the mix was like an extra fun privilege.

The three of us were on top of the ramp's platform discussing how to do this triples run. I explained that my frontside tricks were by far stronger than my backside tricks. So we started flowing in a counterclockwise circular rhythm. Quite a vision to stay focused while being immersed in the middle of this skater cyclone. Produced a dizzying effect, but we all held it together.

Mike McGill is super famous, which to me was obvious. Don Szabo is very famous as well, but not as obvious to me, being I know him on a very personal level and knew him before he was famous. It's like when you're in the picture, it is harder to get a clear view of it, whether the pictures are in color or black and white.

Many times after skate sessions in the hot desert climate, we would refresh ourselves by jumping off this 50 foot bridge into the fresh and cool water of the California Aqueduct. Located only 100 yards away was a down-hill sloped dry drainage ditch which we heavily skated. We would launch off this bridge with our skateboards in hand and pose in stylish aerial stances. Fun aerial dances, until you hit the water. Upon impact, Szabo's board was ripped from his hand, but he swam deeper to the bottom and retrieved it rolling on all four wheels along the bottom of this reservoir. To follow his stunt, I tried to hand stand from the railing of this bridge, but froze in mid rotation. I struck a flat impact into the biggest and loudest back flop of my life, knocking all of the air out of my lungs, once again. Knocking the wind out of myself, I always felt repeating a breath was cheating death.

I was living back in a camper again back in Acton, 20 years since my first residency in this beautiful countryhood. This time around I owned 2 motorcycles, 2 jet skis and 2 dune buggies. So, Szabo and I took one of the buggies out on a restaurant run, quite some distance. By the time we arrived, the throttle pedal was sticking wide open. All we needed to remedy the situation was to apply some kind of lubricant/oil to the throttle pedal. In a joint effort over lunch, we came up with this idea that his salad dressing would do the job. So, we asked our waitress for some oil 'n vinegar to go. Like Mac-Gyver saving the day, making the sticking squeak go away.

Driving a dune buggy is very exhilarating. Giving you the freedom of which you might find driving other vehicles. Stretching my imagination, I could say it's like riding two motorcycles at once, but not. To stretch it a little further, I could visualize the four wheels of the buggy as a skateboard, turning the action in Acton into a conceptualized dirt skatepark, visualizing the contours of cliffs, slopes and banks into an off the wall self-induced hallucination.

Szabo knows what I am talking about when others kind of tune me out during my gravitational experimentational fantasies. Together we have influenced each other's linguistics by trading riddles and rhymes and many times came up with a uniquely congruent vernacular, riddlistic way of communicating.

Don't forget, you won't regret looking up some of Don Szabo's snowboarding work in the "Creatures of Habit" films. His role as "Double OO Szabo" is remarkably accurate to the James Bond movies. Jon Freeman made a series of "Creatures of Habit" videos in the early 90's and Szabo has two very large segments, so don't miss the Double 00 Szabo sequel as well. Freeman is better known for his work that followed, the creation of "Crusty Demons of Dirt" series, which has had a major impact on the world of freestyle motorcross in a legendary way.

Szabo's rockstar lifestyle has had many highs, but like gravity proves again and again, some laws like "what goes up, must come down" are sure to follow. After his snowboarding career, thawed out, he found a beautiful lady named Heather, his soulmate, so they married and settled down into the American dream to raise their two wonderful little girls. Heather's career as a teacher seemed fitting, as she had a charismatic style to her that I'm sure was a blessing to all of her students. I'm sure she taught Don many lessons along the way as well. But, the hardest thing he would have to learn is how to live without her. Cancer sucks! Heather had survived breast cancer and all was looking like they could continue their life living happily ever after. But, it returned with a deep vengeance in the form of Stage 4 bone cancer.

Szabo's shoes always looked pretty comfortable to me, until then. The next steps he was going to take were turning into a long mile. The life he led up until then had conditioned his brain to process very high highs. I believe everyone's scale balances out in the feelings department. For example, the higher you have been the lower you can go, in the opposite direction to the same degree. Now, he was going to have to process the very lowest lows. From what I witnessed from a distance of my close friend, was that his brain did not process the loss for a few years. When it hit his lowest degree (almost off the charts), it hit hard. Depression was an unfamiliar feeling for him and it almost became his demise.

I'm happy to report from several years after the loss of such a wonderful wife, he survived himself. I don't know if one can ever fully recover from such a devastation, but one can only learn how to live again. "Everyone owes life some sort of tragedy", so they say. Well, I would consider his debt paid. Although my friend has endured numerous broken bones that you can put in a cast, a broken heart will last, because in the future you will see the past.

I have spent a great deal of time riding dirt bikes with Damon Huffman. His talents influenced me to a point where when the film crews would show up to make Moto-X freestyle videos, they would include me a well, on his coat tails. For he was the WOW factor and I was more of the OW factor. I would try some of the same cliff climbs as he would, but my attempts usually ended in hilarious disasters. Three different video filming crews found this extremely amusing. I was actually getting paid $200.00 a day plus hotel costs to wipe-out and crash for cash! Crashing came natural to me, and being a skateboarder really helped me get away with rolling out of many situations without major injuries. Time has often clicked into slow motion when I am in the act of regaining balance.

Damon was well known to be humble about his fame; I admired that. I painfully came to realize that "all men are created equal" is very debatable. Now, I realize that in the turf arena, he received a huge gift, and in other arenas like the surf, my gift was bigger. Damon and I went to Hawaii and switched roles as spectators. He stood on the beach the same way I stood in the bleachers to watch him race. Though I never made a penny surfing, except for teaching surf lessons, Damon Huffman on the other hand was one of the first riders in history to sign a million dollar (3-year) contract with Kawasaki.

Before the Supercross races at the stadiums, more than several fans would gather to get his autograph and take pictures with him. Once when I was present, I also was requested to sign autographs and take pictures with some of my fans from the moto videos. My ego saw it as signing a big shot contract. This actually made me ride with more confidence, but my arrogance led me into more crashing.

The three dirt bike videos I had large segments in were ironically named "Throttle Junkies", "Vidiots Anonymous" and "5th Gear Pinned". My name and picture are on the box covers and have been distributed worldwide. This was the mid-90's before the internet had globalized the planet.

The 1990's were a very influential time for the next generation of dirt bikers. Many of them grew up watching us on T.V. over and over until the video tapes wore out. This was pre D.V.D. Many of these little kids grew into the men that pushed the envelope of the extreme sport and many of them became very famous and some of them died doing it.

Thanks to social media, they have occasionally made contact with me and called me a legend. This added to my legendary ego. But, I'm aware of my ego today, and turn the credit over to God.

This life I've led has not been all fun, but far from no fun at all. It has warped my psyche into a shape where I feel comfortable. My eyes see normally unusual things. When I look at a mountain I envision a jump or a line I might roost in the dirt, or picture it covered in snow as I glide my imaginary carve line down the slope. If the landscape of the city is my view, I see obstacles to skate and do tricks from – road trippin' as I maneuver down the highway. An extreme sport extremist can artistically create a psychological playground out of the environment of which he has adapted.

To mention a few of my fleeting moments in the limelight will set the stage of what it was like growing up around a location where so many big screen movies were filmed. Stumbling my way onto the set, I played the part of a surfer in the box office blockbuster "Point Break" in a scene with Keanu Reeves and Gary Busey.

My surfer stereo- type looks also landed me as an extra in a "B" movie named "Summer Fantasy". Jay Adams (if you know the DogTown story), you know of Jay, a truly legendary skater, was also an extra in this made-for-TV movie. Jay caught the eye of the director while we were surfing at Venice Beach during February in freezing water without wetsuits to give the movie that summery vibe. So, the director selected Jay Adams to play the part of an injured surfer. Fake blood was applied to Jay's leg for the scene. I was hoping the sharks would know it was fake. In the movie it looked real.

Being a pool man just outside the Hollywood area, I would often work for rock stars and movie stars, keeping their swimming pools crystal clear. Now, living on the other side of the world in Southeast Asia, I enjoy revisiting my homeland via watching movies on the big screen. So many memories are revived while eating popcorn.

On paper in print, I have also had my fair share of coverage, covering from full page pictures of me flying off my skateboard ramp with my motor- cycle in the "Crash 'n Burn" section of "Dirt Bike" magazine to several video reviews in multiple magazines. My name placed in surf contest results in surfing magazines. Also mentioned in "Transworld Skateboarding" magazine.

Szabo and I together got huge full page pictures in the sports section of the L.A. Times newspaper. I remember the L. A. Times reporter hanging around our Green Sector crew, breaking into the backyards of abandon houses with us to cover the pool skating. This guy really did us justice. It was a great read both times. That's right – twice. Kind of a strange coincidence that they did two separate stories on us that came out exactly one year apart. The dates are the strange part. The third Thursday in July, 1986, then again the third Thursday in July, 1987. I really enjoyed a sense of pride that hit me when I walked into the swimming pool shop of where I just started working. My boss had seen the picture in his newspaper before I had and he hung it on the wall. It was an off the wall experience to see myself on that wall.

A gift that gives you gifts was also something I was experiencing during this time period. Barfoot, Variflex and Z-Flex had all given me skateboards and accessories. I never considered myself officially sponsored with a contract and everything. But, these gifts really kept me in the presence of gratitude. Lip Smack surfboards gave me a surfboard and Prop Snowboards (my most sponsor-like sponsor) was supplying me with lift tickets and snowboards.

I never felt rich and famous, just well-known and getting by. It was truly a magical time for me as everything I put a lot into I got a lot back in return. To stay humble, I need to remember it's not all about me . . . . . but . . . . I was always there. Just be cool, so you can enjoy your own company, because you never go away no matter where you go. When you are alone and become your own company, try not to be your worst company, only your best. You'll never know just how you look through other people's eyes. Just focus on your first-hand view.

Believing in God seems to make life less difficult. Believing you are God, seems to make life more difficult. Free-will allows us to choose what we want to believe. The choice is ours.

Normally Unusual Thoughts"
N.U.T.
"It's a fine line between arrogance and confidence"

After drinking a swimming pool's worth of beer, I sobered up to see past the illusion and came to the conclusion that alcohol gave me an ingenuine sense of superiority. Looking past the distortion of my beer goggles and flexing my beer muscles, I see it did not make me any more intelligent. In fact, often quite the opposite. But, it made Bud-wiser, or so he thought.

It's not that man uses only 10% of their brain. It's that only 10% of mankind uses their brain. I've heard only 1 out of 10 people read books consistently. They say the ego is that little voice inside your head. This is some of mine rambling, like it does 90% of the time.

We always have to be mindful of our mindset or risk getting upset. Try to keep that in mind. Our ego creates a dialog in our head that often keeps us awake at night and is also responsible for a lot of unnecessary suffering. Ego is not necessarily evil, but a necessary requirement for extreme sports to achieve greatness while minimizing injury or death. That is where a fine line is drawn between arrogance and confidence.

First, you have to picture yourself executing a stunt before the action can be achieved. Confidence you will need to complete this foresight. Picture if it you will, then "will it" to become the picture. Belief then produces truth. Doubt can create fear and fear has very little benefit in most situations.

Again, faith over rides fear. The A.A. program has many tools, some of which are acronyms. E.G.O. they say is "Edging God Out". For me what I believe to be true is – talents are God-given. If I took credit for all the things I am capable of doing, it may give me a God-like complex. With extreme sports, these gifts keep you in the present. During the act of a dangerous maneuver if you're not focusing on the present, either regretting the past or fearing the future, you are highly likely to crash. There is very little room for lack of conviction.

CHAPTER 5

"TERRIFIC TRAGEDIES"

"Comical Cosmic Harmony"

My 1st wife and I dated for over a year while waiting until she turned 18 years old to get married. We spent 1990 through 1996 in a marriage that can be best described as punk rock. In the 90's I spent more time riding my dirt bike than her, and I did them both a lot.

The comparison between the dirt bikes and women had crossed my mind; both are fun to ride, but you can really get hurt on them. From what I know, a broken leg heals quicker than a broken heart. My Grandpa Kitchen during his Alzheimer's/Dementia stage once told me "Vince, you are the only man I know that loves motorcycles more than women". That was the last thing I heard him say that made much sense.

Even though our marriage ended tragically, I have to say I would do it again if we could, but of course, differently. Some of our best times were snowboarding together. I would rather not mention our worst times.

I can tell you the beginning of the end was just before the 1994 Northridge earthquake. Our marriage was already getting kind of shaky, but after the quake things really erupted and completely collapsed.

January 17, 1994 at 4:30:55 a.m., we experienced a 6.7 magnitude earthquake, an awakening like no other. Our dogs, Moto and Buddy, were bouncing way above our bed. Moto, a 125 lb. black lab pit-bull mix, landed on me before the shaking had stopped. After knocking him back off the bed, I was able to look out the window south 8 miles to the San Fernando Valley, the epicenter.

Flames and explosions filled the black night sky. Seriously, my first thought was "This is the end." Honestly, Armageddon . . . . . the fires of hell had broken through the surface of the earth to burn us all.

Our double-wide mobile home was knocked off its support jacks and fell 3 feet to the ground. The stairs on the outside of our 3-doored home stayed upright and therefore trapped us inside our home. As I was running through the house looking for a door that would open, I kept tripping over the jacks that had popped through the floor. All gas and water pipes snapped into pieces like twigs. Still totally dark, trying to escape our domain was difficult. I couldn't find a flashlight and luckily couldn't find a match to light a candle because the smell of gas was heavy and I wasn't thinking clearly.

While my mind was still trying to process what had happened, I remember thinking about alcohol. This was during a sober spell in my life, so instead I grabbed a "near beer" (non-alcoholic beverage). The battle in my head was raging and after about a month, I was back on the bottle.

One of the things that drove me back to drinking was that my livelihood cleaning pools was located right in the center of this war-looking zone. Bridges had fallen, streets had cracked in two and many houses were burnt to the ground. My 10 minute commute to work turned into a 3 hour 8 mile drive each way! So many of my pools were beyond repair and I lost almost half my income. Of the pools that had survived, most had brick walls that had fallen into them. It was like fishing for cement blocks for the many hard weeks to follow.

We lived right on the edge of the Santa Clara River which is a dry sand wash 90% of the time. I would regularly ride my dirt bike multiple times per week right out my front yard. Another dream location to live in as a dirt biker. One day after work, I rode my motorcycle deep into the surrounding mountains to get away from all the chaos my life had become. The aftershocks (mini earthquakes) continued for several days after the big one on the 17th (D-Day). These tremors would hit hard and often. As I was riding, skimming across the dirt, I could not feel them under my bike, but I saw many dust clouds coming from the ground. All around, looking like bombs were going off. Equally surreal visions also occurred while I was cleaning pools, the aftershocks would ripple radiant aqua eco effects, on the surface of the water.

It took over 6 months to regain any kind of normalcy. For a few months after the home collapsed, we continued to live in it as totaled as it was. We slept on an air mattress that had a slow leak next to a wood burning stove to get us through the cold winter months ahead. Finally, we put a small camper trailer in the front yard to live in until the insurance company came through on buying us a brand new doublewide 1600 square foot mobile home. So, in the end, we had a nicer home than the one we started with. We went through a lot of shit in the process. And, well as you know, beautiful things need fertilizer to grow. As flowers bloom, all that lives is born to die.

Due to the marital stress or maybe full blown alcoholism, my stomach was experiencing tremendous pain. Turned out it was a near fatal condition with a twist, a unique case of diverticulitis. My stomach was literally tied up in knots. But, looking for the cause to blame was futile to solving this problem.

Result was my colon had wrapped itself around my bladder and was squeezing it to death. The operation required the removal of one-third of my bladder and one foot of my colon. It's gross and scary to imagine the truth about all my guts removed and sitting on the table next to me while the doctor cut and sewed up my intestines.

The aftermath left me with a 14" scar. I was off work for almost 3 months, leaving me with enough time to get the tape measure out and add up my total accumulated scar tissue which I had collected as an extreme sports addict. So, including all my surf, skate, snowboard and Moto-X scars, I had achieved a 27" collection of scar tissue, which I refer to as souvenirs.

While in the hospital, I was not permitted to eat food for eleven days straight. This dropped my weight 25 lbs., bringing me down to the same weight as my dog Moto. I was sick as a dog.

Awakening from the surgery was a nightmare. Hoses, tubes and wires coming out of me and going into me, this way and that. I went into a full blown panic attack as I found it suffocating to breathe with a tube stuck down my throat. This triggered a psychosomatic gag reflex complex that lasted almost 30 minutes. I was trying to scream, but I couldn't physically produce the noise. "Silent" and "listen" use the same letters in spelling, and I felt silent like no one was to listen.   It felt like I was drowning. Similar feeling as to when you get the wind knocked out of you and it feels like your lungs are collapsing.

This over 8-hour operation often leaves people with a temporary and often permanent colostomy bag attached to them. I was the youngest person my surgeon had known that had diverticulitis with my type of complication. I will never forget hearing Dr. Carpenter say, "Being 29 years old you should be able to recover without a colostomy bag". I am forever grateful for his excellent work. I knew my dirt biking days were far from over and his expertise during surgery prevented me from having shit splattering wipe-outs in my future. And, even today, over two decades later, while crashing I keep my shit together, once I catch my breath.

Unfortunately, my marriage wasn't going to bounce back from the shit it was going through. 1994 to 1996 saw 3 major catastrophes. Earthquake, operation and finally a divorce. And a bankruptcy was just around the corner.

These seemed like what might be the worst years of my life, but these years were also filled with many highlights to brighten the dark times. These were also the years I was filming dirt bike videos and enjoying that limelight alongside my fast and famous friends.

By 1997 I had realized alcohol might kill me and then I wouldn't be able to drink or even breathe anymore. They say, "If you are truly an addict/ alcoholic, there will come a time you stop drinking/using. It is just better to be alive when that time arrives".

For me, alcohol always seemed more dangerous than drugs. I was able to stop drinking for a while by using lots of drugs to quench my thirst. But, this theory enraged my appetite for more drugs. Still, I thought my chances for survival were better substituting alcohol with drugs. Many people say alcohol is not a drug. The political paperwork has told society it is acceptable. Ultimately, alcohol is a drug.

My return to psychedelics was fun at first. I had not been doing any of those since the high school days on purple haze. For the previous 10 years or so it was only massive daily doses of beer and pot.

Ecstasy was very popular around 1997, but very expensive, over $20.00 a pill. Some days I would take as many as four. The path I was following lead me to a new, more economical synthetic designer drug named Gamma Hydroxybutyrate, also known as Liquid-X. Liquid ecstasy also had negative side effects such as sweating, loss of consciousness, nausea, hallucinations, amnesia, coma and a few others. It was a schedule III(3) controlled substance that I was acquiring via the black market. In the end, I didn't save much money.

For some reason I can't explain I was still able to clean pools while totally wasted on this stuff. In A.A./N.A., some of us are referred to as functioning alcoholics/addicts. Well, I went one step further and considered myself a productive alcoholic/addict.

Here is why for example. Early one morning while cleaning a pool high on G.H.B. (Liquid-X), I started talking with the customer and she decided to call an ambulance due to my peculiar behavior. By the time they got there to take me to the hospital, I was still feeling great and had a slightly firmer grip on the realms of reality than earlier.

Upon their arrival, I tried to explain that I was fine, but my communication skills were still incomprehensible to most the earthlings on the planet. So, for a demonstration of my capabilities, I started walking on my hands upside down, down their front yard stairway. See, balance in check, no need for your assistance! Thank you!

I ended up in the ambulance and spent 3 to 4 hours in the hospital with electrical monitoring wire connected between me and a machine. They released me and I called a friend to pick me up. We shared a joint as he drove me back to my truck with enough light in the day so I finished cleaning the pool. See, I am a productive addict.

That same evening, I remembered I had a date with a really cute lady. I picked her up and we saw the newest Star Wars movie. I remember thinking as we were watching the movie, man this day has been more spaced out than this movie. In reflection, my life was in another galaxy as well.

Another time I was really high on this synthetic designer drug. I went out to lunch with my friend, Tyler, and his wife Lisa and their 3 year old daughter. This drug would produce energy, lots of speed-like energy. My whole body would tense up. Steroid-like effects; that's why so many body builders also got hooked on this drug. Anyhow, I'm sitting there holding my glass of water so extremely tight that it shattered and an explosion of glass covered our table.

Lisa, bless her heart, got scared and got up to take their daughter to a safer table. Tyler and I stayed there while he drank his beer and I ordered another water thinking in my twisted mind, "at least I'm not drinking alcohol – that stuff is dangerous".

Occasionally, I would take up laying on the customer's diving boards while cleaning their pools. Usually nobody was home and I had their back-yards all to myself. Looking back on it now, I realize I would have lost my job if I wasn't self-employed working as the Water Wizard. Being your own boss is bitchen. Also, in recollection, I am lucky to be alive.

To me, there is very little difference between Alcoholics Anonymous and Narcotics Anonymous. Both are 12-Step programs. So, I sought survival in A.A. and N.A. for more than the next decade. Yet, I was unable. I should say unwilling to stay clean and sober. I kept reaching 3 months, 6 months and even a few 8 months sustained. I could never get a full year clean and sober. As they say I was a "slipper" and a slippery slipper I was, but luckily I never quit quitting. While coming and going in and out of the program, more crazy things kept happening in between my time of dabbling with sobriety.

Lucky again, I was not drinking on this day, nevertheless the drugs almost killed me a couple of times during that 24-hour period. I woke up next to a girlfriend. She had 4 children and the youngest one needed a ride to school, so I volunteered.

Before I left to do a good deed for my girlfriend, I saw she had some blue little pills near the bed. Upon my request, she gave me some. I wasn't familiar with those at the time, but when I took Vicodin I usually took 4 at a time. Popping 4 at a time turns out to be way too many with Xanax.

As I was driving her daughter to school, the pills kicked in hard. I started banking off parked cars, tearing a few side view mirrors off in the process. Before anything too major happened, I dropped her off at school, shaken up, but safe. Actually, dropped her off a little before we reached the school, upon her request.

A couple of things to be grateful for already, first of all, she didn't get hurt. Secondly, her father was an outlaw biker who ran with the Mongrels, a notoriously violent biker gang. They would have seriously hurt me if I had harmed his daughter.

I was getting coma-like sleepy from that point going to my house 30 minutes away. Well, I was destined to be unconscious before that amount of time passed anyway. When I awoke, I was 100 feet from my truck, which was completely totaled. It was wedged underneath a huge gasoline hauler 18-wheeler semi-truck.

The police officer was holding my head up saying something like

"Are you on a substance?" So, I answered with a question, "Why?" He said, "Because you are acting incredibly calm considering what just happened."

I actually believe I might have slipped into a never-ending sleep that comes to many who take a large quantity of Xanax. That crash had violently awoken me, luckily. I had chipped a tooth and had stitch-worthy cuts on my face. I never wear seat belts; still don't. The air bag was really useful.

Luckily, or maybe not so lucky, this time I went to the hospital instead of jail. There they stitched me up and released me with some Vicodin to take for the pain.

So, I popped 4 every hour instead of 1 every 4 hours. Sometimes that's how dyslexics read things, which also is very common for an addict. Going forward, backwards is often more than just directions.

I don't remember how, but I made it to my street bike. Got on my Honda Shadow 600cc and rode to a friend's house to score some more pot, because my stash was hidden in the truck I had just totaled. Later in the week, I would visit the junkyard to reconnect with that hidden dope.

That same night after smoking several bongloads, I was walking backwards down my friend's driveway toward my motorcycle telling him how I was really walking forward because the planet was rotating from east to west. As I was explaining this profound perception, I tripped on a crack in the sidewalk causing me to crack the back of my head wide open leaving blood on the streets again.

Now I had cracks on both sides of my cranium, which was spinning like a globe in full twirl in a galaxy of its own. Still in full spin, I wanted to get home. Home was a camper parked 20 minutes away up a dark and winding canyon road and then through a long dirt road up into the mountains of Acton. Luckily my friend snatched my keys from me and made me leave my motorcycle at his house while he gave me a ride home.

Next morning when I woke up to clean my pools, I had no truck and no bike. I did have two new souvenirs from the prior day's activities on the front and back side of my skull. I approached the day still buzzing with excitement from the previous day's experiences!

Determined to get to work, I hitch-hiked a ride 30 minutes to the closest rent-a-car, rented a truck and cleaned my pools. As you remember, I am a productive alcoholic/addict. Plus, I was my own boss and didn't want to let myself down. But, in all truthfulness, that day I was more of a danger to society than a productive member of society.

Many times I would give up on my efforts for better living through chemistry and return to alcohol, both potions to alter emotions. In these times of personal survey studies, I would find drugs to be more convenient and the application much less time consuming. Just popping a pill or smoking a couple of hits only takes minutes at the most. Whereas alcohol practically handicapped me to a one-handed efficiency, while always needing the other hand to hold my drink.

Once I started drinking I could never get any work done. Instantly I would become lazy spiked with crazy and turned my view of reality hazy. Alcohol also gave me tragically terrible hangovers. I was a puker. I have actually thrown up so many times that I could have filled up a jacuzzi. In effect, I caused permanent damage to my esophagus and for the rest of my life I will be taking medication to prevent myself from throwing up. I linked my G.E.R.D. (gastroesophageal-reflux disease) to my alcoholism.

Here is a cautionary tale to tell of an experience I had during a time of switching back to alcohol to replace drugs.

One day I got on my KTM 525 Moto-X/street legal motorcycle with a pack strapped to my back. I had gone clothes shopping with the intentions of filling my backpack with new apparel and returning home to my camper.

I had just returned to the United States after surfing and living in Costa Rica for the whole year of 2007. I was working and living in an R. V. storage yard named Playtime R.V. in Oxnard, California.

So, after filling my backpack with new threads, I decided to pick up a bottle of 100 proof vodka and visit a strip club.

My Spanish was pretty good by then and I made a new friend named Sancho, an illegal alien from Mexico here to pick the harvest that grows in Oxnard, California. We traded enough Spanish words to decide we wanted to play billiards while still being able to see naked titties. So, I said, "Follow me in your car to Snooky's. That strip club has a pool table." He must have known where it was because he was already there when I finally showed up. Somehow I got lost while popping wheelies on my motorcycle, trying to show off for my new found friend, who I thought was watching. But his eyes made it back to the visions of titties before I even realized I was lost.

I remember Sancho being on the skinny and short side and having really bad breath. And, what was coming out of my mouth was belligerent, bi-lingual babel. With all this half comprehensible gibberish I was spitting out, I was making a few new enemies in this low-bottom bar as I was pushing the patience of the manager and bouncer. At this time I should have left already. But, then two of the strippers got into a cat fight in the corner of the bar. No one noticed at first until I had already jumped in to break them up. By the time everyone had noticed, it looked like I was in the middle of this fight with the strippers. It didn't look good; I was misinterpreted.

The bouncer grabbed me by my backpack and swung me around. When the room quit spinning, I saw Sancho ready to back me up with his beer muscles. Anyhow, I readily agreed to leave. But, by then someone had called the police and had the nerve to tell me that the cops were on their way to get me.

Heartbeat pounding rapidly now. This news prompted me to get on my bike as fast as I could, so I would be gone before their arrival. As fate had it, my motorcycle wouldn't start. The starter battery was too low, but it would still bump start. So, I asked for one final favor from my compadre, and as he pushed me out the driveway and onto Pacific Coast Highway, that was the last I saw of Sancho.

The next thing I saw was multiple cop cars with lights and sirens flashing and blasting behind me. It was less than a quarter mile to Playtime R.V. Center (storage yard) where I lived and worked. So, I gassed it full throttle hoping to make it there before they could catch up to me. They stopped at the crowd of people in front of Snooky's to investigate the situation. This bought me about half a minute or so before fingers started pointing in my direction. This was just enough time for me to make it to the security gate and get my clearance card into the slot that opened the gate.

At that point, at gun point, I was surrounded by 3 or 4 police cars. As they separated my backpack from me and me from my motorcycle, they were the first ones to see my new clothes as they searched my backpack. I was handcuffed and sitting on the curb still speaking in my broken Spanish, when I should not have been talking at all. I had the right to remain silent, but I did not have the ability.

I can picture this scene in my memory perfectly, because I saw the scene as it was happening in the reflection of the Playtime headquarters, a huge 2-story building covered with reflective glass walls. Here, I identified myself as the all night security watchman of the 7 acres, which I oversaw/ maintained over 300 motorhomes, one of them being my home.

I couldn't prove that I was innocent, but I could prove that I was already home. Luckily, I had made it that far before negotiations had begun. I explained, this time in English that I was just trying to do the right thing and stop the violence that had occurred between the two dancers. And through some more unexplainable luck, they let me push my bike through the storage yard gate and go to sleep.

Had I gone to jail, there would have been no way to follow through with the plans I had for the following day. Waking up was painful. All the aspirin in the world wouldn't fix this headache from hell. And, in just an hour, my parents were bringing my young nieces and nephews to my home on wheels so we could all spend the day at the beach as planned. So, we all piled into my motorhome and I drove us to the beach.

I have pictures of that day, skim-boarding with my family. The pictures look like I'm enjoying myself as much as they were. But, after getting chased the night before while chasing the wrong kind of fun, all I could do was to bear my existence that day. The fresh cold ocean water helped a little, but even under water, it felt like my head was inside out and my stomach outside in.

A.A./N.A. provides real friends for a lifetime worldwide, a universally felt common bond comparable to the kind survivors of a shipwreck share. We all had to survive ourselves from a sort of self-indulgent drowning, almost a suicidal manslaughter. Floating around the world like a message in a bottle, we carry the message we needed to be able to put the bottle down. This man helped me stay afloat. Ronnie was one of many of my sponsors in this program, along this voyage.

Just because someone gives you advice doesn't mean he is more intelligent than you. It may mean he has done enough stupid stuff to make him wise. Some of the most memorable wisdom is earned through shocks and burns. One piece of wisdom Ronnie shared with me was to picture my ego as a balloon. The bigger it is inflated, the easier it is to burst. So, I try to keep mine property inflated nowadays.

I met Ronnie in 2003 at an A.A. meeting. We share more than one common interest; he is also a surfer. I couldn't stay sober for the next 8 years, going in and out of the program, but we continued our friendship nevertheless. Even between my times of experimenting with sobriety, Ronnie was always there. He never gave up on me even when I gave up on giving up. Even when my addiction put him in jeopardy.

In 2005, Ronnie and I and a few others from the A.A./N.A. program went to Mexico to surf and celebrate a bachelor party. During this time period

I was off the alcohol, but wherever I went my drugs were also coming along for the trip.

Crossing an international border is always a location for high anxiety, especially carrying a controlled substance which can render you some jail time. Sneaky and clever-like, I snuck some pot in without my five clean and sober friends' acknowledgment. Really proud of myself for picking the perfect hiding spot for my stash. Concealed inside a watertight aspirin bottle which I placed under the hood next to the engine inside the window wiper fluid container. So, so far so good.

We drove an hour or so past the border with both my friends and the authorities none the wiser. We checked into a hotel and got some tacos. I noticed a pharmacy across the street and knew prescriptions were not necessary in this country, so I stocked up on some pills. But, what I didn't know is exactly what they were going to do. Much like myself at the time. This was before I learned how to speak Spanish and the pharmacist's information I received was lost in translation. Anyhow, I soon found out the pills produced a lousy buzz and a stomach ache as I proceeded to sweat a lot.

The night went on as many bachelor parties do. A night of south of the border shenanigans gave way to the sunrise. Without any sleep that I can remember, we got in my truck with the surfboards unlawfully hanging out a few feet past the tailgate. This gave the policia a reason to pull us over. I believe it was discrimination considering that the truck in front of us had chicken coops, a refrigerator and a very long ladder hanging out way past their tailgate.

Just the same, the surfer shake down began. I don't blame them. Any cop getting paid 3rd world wages is going to be looking for bribes to feed their brides and tribes. This was not the first time this has happened to me, nor was it going to be the last. Of course, we were not going to pay much for boards sticking out too far. Though this was a reason, or I should say their excuse to stop us.

My friends were still clueless about my stashed marijuana. But, by this time though, I had moved it from the ultra-safe spot to under the backseat inside the tire jack compartment for easier access when I needed to sneak a hit. So, as the policia are doing their shake down and search procedures, they kept looking at my red, white and blue blood shot eyes. At the same time my innocent friends appeared fairly relaxed. Unlike them, my paranoid behavior was giving me away once my anxiety levels got too high. And just as the cop was grabbing the lever to the tire jack compartment, I handed his hand a $100 bill and the search was over, just like that.

We finally got in the ocean and surfed. Often, I have felt safer swimming with sharks in the water than interacting with man on land.

After a while, I told my friends the truth. In that pack I was the black sheep with a white lie. See, you can twist the truth and say you are sober because you are not drinking alcohol, but true sobriety means freedom from all substances which affect you from the neck up. Throughout large portions of my life, I was torn up from the floor up and needed a checkup from the neck up.

My friends were all clean and sober, but still they almost went to jail because of my addiction. Later, Ronnie told me that if we all had ended up in jail, he would have kicked my ass harder than anyone else could have in that Mexican jail. And, I would have deserved it.

Ronnie is 10 years my elder and a big brother in my eyes. I can see clearly now that his example of sobriety has helped clear the path. Luckily, I still get to see him via video calls and visit him when I'm in the U.S.A. He always says, "Friends for life, right?!" I see him as a lifer in the world of sobriety and partly because of him I see myself the same way.

"Normally Unusual Thoughts"""

N. U. T.

**"Any society that would give up a little liberty
to gain a little security, will deserve neither and lose both"
- Benjamin Franklin**

It seems that war and conflict come when the countries' mindsets (ideologies) clash, making things diff-cult (different-cult)

Since I have entered a realm of reality where nothing never happens, I have found constant entertainment where the possibilities are never ending and often random. I have tried changing the world. After finding that impossible, I found it possible to change how I see the world.

**"We don't see things as they are; we see them as we are"
- Anais Nin**

The amount of books I have read has reached the triple digits, including every page of the Bible. The locations I have resided have exceeded two dozen addresses. This is my resume to being book smart as well as street smart. I don't say this to brag or claim brilliance. I am just saying I have seen the same things from many different angles, thanks to being well traveled as well as well read.

I have lived amongst three drastically different cultures around the world. My world view is tinted through the mindset my subculture has given me as a skater/surfer. Maybe I am normally unusual, but I see a hidden message in the first four letters of culture (cult). I think there is more to it than just a play on words.

What I've read has affected how I write and where I've lived has affected how I live. Culture or our cult has a profoundly powerful effect on controlling our thoughts and influencing our actions. Traditions and conditioned mindsets keep us stuck in this unnoticed yet highly influenced frame of mind which we inherit from our country's ancestors.

The catch is people. "People, you can't live with them and you can't live without them". Culture is inescapable from the outside, but freedom can be found from the inside. By releasing outside reasoning and rethinking through our own reasoning to create our own beliefs. Our reasoning, or at least our perception of it, is a product of our experiences. A personal reality if you will. No two persons' experiences are the same, each one is unique and normally unusual. We should have the right to shape our own personal reality, within reason, and have personal experiences without the need of another's permission.

Having genuine relationships are difficult when an inferior (in-fear-of) and a superior try to have a mutual understanding. A lot of authenticity is lost until the roles can be dropped and an equal sense of worth is acquired. By escaping segregation, people can see eye to eye. This would create an ego-less bond that could help form truly genuine relationships. A problem with a culture of which a government's influence is that they easily force their beliefs onto society. This is where our freedom is at jeopardy. War and other devastating problems occur when egos attempt to control other people's beliefs.

My philosophy has to do with the psychology of spirituality, which may be the answer to global stability. In my search and research of enlightenment, I have found stability in almost every aspect of my life, which has seen its fair share of chaos.

America, Costa Rica and the Philippines are all completely different in their general mindsets (ideologies). The opinions I have of these three places are the impressions they left on me during my experiences living immersed in their cultures. The least impressionable was the U.S.A. because my mindset was rooted there from birth and that is what seems normal to me.

Considering the year I lived in Costa Rica was approached fearlessly, that sure influenced my impression. "Excuse me while I kiss the sky" was my attitude going in and I walked away with the impression that the sky had kissed my brain and in return soothed my soul. A soul of a soul surfer would feel right at home here. I felt at home living there, but as my past proves, I've never been able to stay at home too long.

When I lived C.R., I seldom wore a shirt due to the extreme heat being located on the equator and only wore shoes when I skateboarded. Surprisingly, my feet grew one full shoe size that year. No restriction permits growth. This is a perfect example of a metaphor. You may have heard people in Costa Risa live almost stress free and are very happy. This I found true, due to my experience. There are very few restrictions there, and there is where I found freedom from my head to my toes.

In the same year that the Philippines ruled that the punishment for a man shirtless in public would be jail time, America passed a law in six of their states that women are allowed in public shirtless. This is good news to some people, bad news to others. I guess I particularly found this frustrating considering that half the time I was cleaning pools, was spent shirtless. My past influencing my opinion, again.

The differences between the cultures are the different stories, each inherited through their own heritage. Each ideology is uniquely made up. Despite the excessive discipline in the Philippines, the people I meet here appear to be some of the happiest people I've ever met.

Americans really take their freedom for granted. I didn't realize the extent of that freedom until I experienced the contrast. The U.S.A. is a collection of mixed nuts; a bunch of different cultures mixed into a blender to stir things up.

"The further a society drifts from the truth, the more it will hate those who speak it."
~ George Orwell

A lot of things can be foreseen as tragic. It helped me once I read that "85% of the things we worry about never actually happen, and the 15% that do happen turn out not to be as terrible as we had imagined they would be". Therefore, as we suffer a hundred tragedies, eighty-five of them happened solely in our heads.

Trippy as the world turns, it can make your head spin. It made by head turn when I realized anger is caused by fear. Anger is madness. It's crazy how fast fear can drive you mad. But, fear is only fear (False Evidence Appearing Real). Faith is the anecdote that stops the spinning.

"Those who are able to see beyond the shadows and lies of their culture will never be understood, let alone believed by the masses".
- Plato

CHAPTER 6

"I   K.W.I.T."

"I Know What I Think"

Thirteen years of my visit on earth I spent living in another ideal location, 1992-2005 in Canyon Country, California. I owned my own home in a trailer park while exchanging the cost of my space rent for cleaning the park's pool. This was the 3rd time I had managed to get paid for cleaning my own pool. Ideal address for my lifestyle, dirt biking right out the door and located equal distances between surfing and snowboarding.

I've always felt right at home being in the middle of the action. On the map I was seated 20 minutes southwest of Acton. I had envisioned myself paying off the 20 year mortgage and retiring in this spot. My vision couldn't foresee God's view or why this address would one day be wiped off the map. You will have to stay tuned to see how that unfolds.

Through some footage in the dirt bike video "Throttle Junkies", the evolution of the rock band "I K.W.I.T." had formed and lasted 8 years. Damon Huffman evolved to the bass guitar, but started out banging on a makeshift drum kit that I had made from a bunch of empty chlorine barrels, swimming pool equipment and a real drum symbol hanging from the ceiling on a rope. I cut a broomstick into pieces for drumsticks. Next to him I played my electric guitar and screamed into a microphone. This created a noise that when most people heard it, they wished we would quit.

Our meaning and spelling for the band, I K.W.I.T. stands for "I know what I think". After the band got washed up and the sounds settled to dust, we changed the meaning to past tense I.K.W.I.T. standing for "I know what

I thought". Some of the old songs and lyrics still bounce around in my head with a rhythm and rhyme from time to time.

So, not only was this a house of music, it also was a home to constant fun. A perfect place for all my extreme sports wants and needs. My space #70 was located at the very end of the park. But, now the map only shows 69 mobile homes in the Sand Canyon Mobile Home Park. It was by far the biggest lot in the park and measured out at very close to 1/3 of an acre. The front yard was huge. Just on the other side of my fence was the Santa Clarita river bed.

In 1998 a huge storm filled the river and swallowed 20' by 90' of my yard still leaving me with an unusually big mobile home space. The mobile home itself was 1,600 square feet and was a brand new custom ordered home. It replaced the original 1975 doublewide that I had bought in 1992 as I have mentioned after the 1994 earthquake had collapsed the 1st one. I was left with this one in 1995. My wife had vacated in 1996, so I had this extremely spacious place and space to just be me.

Being a poolman supplied me with enough money to fill this place with every toy my imagination wanted. Within a few years, my home was stocked with a pool table, deluxe drum set, piano, PlayStation, a big screen T.V. and in my yard I installed a Jacuzzi and also had a garage built for my many motorcycles. I never had awakened from my dream to "Board to Death" so I built two skateboard half pipe ramps on my property over the years. With some leftover used wood, I even built a treehouse in one of the 7 trees. I was blessed to have this land.

All this existed as a fantasy that was now my reality. Fresh air out my front door with mountainous horizons surrounding the desert-like atmosphere. The house itself contained more square footage than I could utilize, so I rented out the two front rooms to Tim Tolleson, a.k.a. (Lump). Lump was photographer and the managing editor for "Dirt Bike Magazine" at the time. It was great to have him living there. I always had someone to ride with.

Lump is a true motorhead and we would ride great trails together several times every week. I kind of felt bad when the band "I KWIT" got loud and we always got loud. So loud that my ears would often ring after sessions. It must have been difficult for Lump at times, maybe every time.

One sunny day, Lump and I were riding through a drainage tunnel too small for a car to drive through. If you didn't duck, your helmet would scrape the ceiling. This tunnel went under Hwy 14 freeway. We used it often to access great riding trails in the mountains. Surprising to us, we rolled up on this nude dude out of his mind, rubbing mud all over his naked body. We just looked at him, then at each other and just kept on rolling. The man didn't appear capable of having a conversation, so there was really no need to stop. I'm sure Lump remembers this as well as I do and it's something that that guy is probably still trying to forget.

These were very exciting times for us. Damon Huffman (Huffdaddy), Jason Marcus (Nut), Paul Silva (Punkrock Paul), Wayne Byrne (Wayniac) and I (Vertical) were the prominent members that started I KWIT. Along the way many others would randomly jam out with the band from time to rhyme.

After band practice one stormy day, with the rain on and off, we rode. Through the window of opportunity, we the band members and Lump jumped on our bikes to tear up some trails. We were in for a wet and wild ride. When the moisture of the dirt is just right, it creates a chocolate cake texture, this type of dirt is also known to us as "ego dirt", because it would enable us to ride to the maximum of our potential, which would impress ourselves. But, when it was too wet, we called it "slippery as snot". Lump being on the heavy side referred to his disposition as an advantage as it would provide extra traction in some conditions. Our dialog had a definition of its own; we would create terminology for situations constantly.

So the bunch of us are riding that afternoon as the storm's magnitude increased to include lightning and thunder with heavy downpours of cold rain, exhilarated with strong winds. Things were getting intense and to add to the dramatic climate was the fact that it was going to be pitch black dark, as night was coming on quickly. We thought we could find a shortcut back to the trailer park if we left the trail and just cut across a few mountains to save time.

Drum roll please . . . . . this next part gets real intense and surreal. Jason, our drummer, slips at high speed and his crash resulted in breaking his handle bar in two. This is an extremely rare circumstance. Luckily, it was the left side with the clutch cable dangling like a leash attached to the left grip connecting the amputated part of the handle bar. This happened right at the bottom of a monstrous hill climb that was essential to our making it home before dark. To add more excitement, by this point, we were trespassing.

Jason is a very strong man, but this would take much more than sheer strength to accomplish. With lightening striking and thunder exploding, it was now dark enough that the lightening lit up the mountain. This provided Jason with enhanced vision to attack the climb. He had to try, try and try again as the 3rd time was a charm. His coordination and riding skills were of a magical capability that evening. While the throttle was still attached to the right side of the handle bar connected to the bike, the left grip with the clutch was by his side pressed up against his hip. Anyone who has ridden a dirt bike up a huge steep hill knows how much finesse is required on the clutch in that situation.

This was some of the most dramatic dirt biking my eyes will ever see. The sight, the sound, the feel, even the smells are hard to replicate with words, even a picture or video wouldn't do this experience justice. When Nut finally made it to the top and completed his handful of a challenge, we all yelled and screamed cheers of admiration!

Another dirt bike adventure that is engraved into my memory is the time I almost drowned on my motorcycle. Or, I should say with my motorcycle on me. A day after the rainstorm and the streams had a foot or so of water running through them, a dozen or so of us were riding from my home, most of them in front of me, with no looking back. Luckily, Szabo was behind me to get my back.

It was a cold day and we were only a few minutes into a 3 hour ride. I blindly rolled over a hill that had a backside to it a few days before the rain. The now fully flowing stream had eroded the backside of the hill, leaving a 10 foot cliff for me to fly over my handlebars face first into the freezing water.

225 lbs. of motorcycle landed straight on my back, knocking the wind out of me. Breathing was going to be impossible anyhow, now that my bike was holding my face under water. Within a minute, I was breathing again and managed to tilt my head enough to catch a gulp of oxygen. But, I was still pinned under my bike, until Szabo saved the day by lifting the motorcycle off of me.

I wanted to go back to my house and change into a dry set of riding gear, but we had to catch up to the rest of the pack. So, we got back on our bikes and screamed down the riverbed in 5th gear pinned (60 mph). The chill factor was freezing, but in a few miles my clothes had blown dry. And, I felt extra grateful to be breathing the fresh crisp clean air for the rest of the day.

Conveniently from my front porch, Paul Punkrock lived right across the Santa Clarita river bed, being one of my closest friends, geographically. We spent a lot of time together. Partying a lot in between extreme sports scenarios and jam sessions rocking out, we shared many belly aching laughs. Sometimes when he was between jobs, he would help me clean some of my very dirty, windblown swimming pools.

Paul played a powerful rhythm guitar while I simultaneously played the lead guitar. On nights when the rest of the band couldn't get together, we made a groovin' duo. The sounds we made in the mountains together on our dirt bikes also still rings in my head. A biker's ears turn motors into music, riffs and revs.

One moist dirt day just the two of us were riding in Acton bouncing a revved-out sound with our motors between the canyon walls deep in this secluded valley, when things got turned upside down. I had high-sided it and my bike landed right on top of me. This was starting to become a habit. But this time, the motor kept running causing the chain to still spin the back tire, which was right above my head, leaving thick skid marks on my helmet. Paul saw what was happening and quickly came to my rescue to shut my motor off and then release me from the heavy weight of my bike.

This reminds me of another story where Paul rescued me again. Again, releasing me from some heavy weight that was crushing my body. This was during a short period of total sobriety I was getting through. He invited me to come with him and some of his friends to a party up in Frazier Park. We pulled up to a redneck paradise party way up in the mountains.

A desert metal band was jamming loud inside the house. I managed to stay sober, but my thirst for excitement needed to be quenched. As the night went on, these hillbillies got smashing drunk. Most of the party moved outside into the darkness of the cold night to watch these really big bearded dudes have these aggressive, but half playful wrestling matches. I got an idea to make something exciting even more exciting, so I set fire to a wadded paper towel and threw it right between these two bearded hillbillies.

Well, they got excited and after they extinguished their beards, everything just stopped and everybody starting looking at me. Right before a bull charges, there is a standstill moment of impending doom, some say "a deer in the headlights". It was starting to look like "lights out" for me.

I just froze as the quarter ton of hillbillies started charging me. Both of them slammed me into the ground with a thud! I was almost sure that this was the end of my existence. But as soon as the pounding began, it stopped. Paul is big, but not in comparison to these two bearded, or should I say now half-bearded bad asses. Nevertheless, he put a stop to my extinction.

Punkrock Paul is no stranger to danger. I've seen him get his ass kicked from the immense impact that followed some of his motorcycle crashes. He had taken a lickin' and kept on kickin'. A truly great friend and the song goes on.

Adrenaline fixations are not free, but free the soul.

Professional level drummer, Wayne Byrne, was born the same year I was in 1966 as many of my friends were. Dirt in every direction, we would ride. Wayne knew more about dirt in many ways than most dirt bikers do. This was due to his knowledge of farming. Growing everything organic through the dirt and even raising his own chickens and eggs, though I don't remember which one came first.

Wayne believed more in homeopathic remedies than pharmaceutical solutions. Yet, he was the first of my friends to have a heart attack. This happened while he was surfing. I didn't hear from him for a while, but heard a story of medics cutting the wetsuit off his body. Now, he has stints near his heart. He also has a big heart metaphorically and is one of the very few friends I have gone to church with. Wayne is a great family man to his wife and they have raised two wonderful daughters.

Wayne's truly an incredibly talented drummer, but his true profession is concrete cutting. I have always had a great respect for manual labor, being I also chose that, in the form of cleaning pools. I can relate to that type of fatigue that comes with working outside in the elements.

So, one night out of the blue, he is at his friend's house and they are jamming some groovin' beats and you will never guess who showed up? Eddie Vedder. Eddie was one of his friend's friends. Well, there you have it! Wayne Byrne drumming for Eddie Vedder's legendary vocals. A one night only spontaneous event. The speakers that night belonging to Wayne, they each stood near 5 feet tall. These same speakers eventually found a home in my house for several years, where "I KWIT" always jammed. I always found it nostalgic that the same speakers I sang through as the singer for "I KWIT", Eddie Vedder of "Pearl Jam" had also made music through.

Wayne and I used to have mind stimulating discussion, which simulated into intellectual pushing matches. Pushing our perceptions of universal reality.

One day Wayne, Paul and I were jamming and out the window across the sandwash was a huge wildfire up on the hillside. I have always regretted not taking a picture of this scene; it was so surreal and dynamic. We all got excited and thought it would be even more exciting if we hiked up that hill to get closer to the fire. Hot, super hot as we got closer, we began to see wildlife running in the opposite direction. Rabbits, coyotes and deer knew better than we did that day. It finally got too hot, so we had to turn around.

Even spiders were looking for a way out. As a survival technique a sometimes fatally poisonous brown recluse spider jumped on my unknowing leg. I don't know if the stowaway lived or not, and a week later I wasn't sure if I was going to. The poison was in my left leg above my knee and my skin was beginning to fall off in that area. The swelling was extreme, a fist –sized lump of puss was painfully rising day by day. Paul stuck a syringe into my leg trying to empty the poison in a futile attempt. Finally the poison felt like it was entering my brain, so I went to a proper doctor. The clinic confirmed that it was a bite from a brown recluse and gave me proper treatment. My previous self-diagnosis assumed that it was a case of premature rigor mortis.

I'm still alive, but it feels like that little section of my leg is dead and is still numb. Life is a killer. As Jim Morrison of "The Doors" said, "No one gets out of here alive". But as Eddie Vedder of Pearl Jam said, "I'm still alive".

In between songs, this time as a trio, Damon Huffman, Jason Marcus and I went out to the Mojave Desert to ride dirt bikes. Normally we go exploring for about 3 hours before our gas tanks are near empty. I don't remember much about those first 3 hours, except that it was a very dry and hot day, though I will never forget how it ended.

Sometimes the desert starts to look the same in every direction, especially in the really flat areas. Damon and Jason made it back to the truck, tired and dusty thinking their day of riding was done. I drifted off a bit out of alignment with my 2 friends and missed sighting the truck as I kept on the throttle. While I headed off toward a flat horizon, my buddies soon realized their day of riding dirt bikes was not over yet.

After they quickly ate their sandwiches and refueled their gas tanks, they went off in search of Vince. I soon realized I was lost, and soon after that, gas was just a fume in my tank. There were only a couple of hours of light left in the day and the desert gets very cold at night in the land of extremes.

Pushing the dead weight of my motorcycle through the thick dry sandy dirt tired my already extremely fatigued body out and my mind wasn't doing so well either. Once again, I realized I had put my life in jeopardy. My friends burnt through another whole tank of gas just looking for me for another 3 hours, well into the blackness of night. Meanwhile, I spotted a homestead, a single-wide trailer home in the middle of nowhere. I sensed some relief because pushing the motorcycle became easier on the dirt road leading to the home of hope.

A very nice elderly couple let me into their home where I used their phone and drank some water. This was in the mid-1990's before everyone had G.P.S. and cell phones and for them it was still a rotary phone. I knew Damon's mom's phone number on a push button phone. I guess my mind had memorized the push button pattern through muscle memory, but I couldn't successfully use a rotary dial phone at the time. So, my solution was to write down on paper the numbers of a push button phone and let my fingers do the walking to access some talking. It worked. I was able to leave a message for Damon, but no way for him to receive it. The nice folks told me that the highway was a short distance down their access road.

I started pushing in the right direction. Unfortunately my mind was not going in the right direction, nor had it been during the push through the sun backed desert, contemplating my future.

Deep and firmly in the darkness of my thoughts I had promised myself that if I lived I would drink alcohol again. I had been sober for a few months at the time. Well, a promise is a promise and either way I was going to break one.

I finally made it to the highway and now I was on a mission to get drunk. So, I hid my bike 50 feet from the highway behind some cactus and began to hitchhike to the nearest liquor store. Pretty soon I was in line at an AM/PM Minimart, but I had no money. Luckily or maybe unluckily, I had a very expensive pocket knife with me, which I sold to the first buyer for beer money and enough change to operate a pay phone. Luckily Damon was checking in with his mom occasionally to see if I had made contact. Eventually our trio reunited at the gas station and we went back to retrieve my motorcycle.

When thinking deep enough, I realize I was as Ozzy Osborne puts it, "Killing myself to live". Anyhow this is also another reason we named our band "I KWIT" because I was always "quitting" pot and alcohol. Eventually I quit quitting once I stopped starting. I know what I think now, but then I knew what I thought.

The 3 stages of life: 1) You make things happen 2) You watch things happen 3) You wonder what happened.

I knew if I didn't die and it seemed like I just wasn't supposed to yet. I would one day be really old. I have not been one for planning ahead and that has come with a cost. Living in the moment seems to consume most of my time. A priceless expense at that. This was my idea of investing in my future. I knew the stage of life for spectating would be more enjoyable if I had participated in the things I would someday only be watching. I wanted to truly relate to the racing experience. In 2002 I entered the Golden State Series, which consists of racing at 6 different Moto-X tracks across Southern California. Not only did I want to experience racing, I wanted to experience winning! As I make my way from a trophy to atrophy.

Never was I as fast as most of my friends. A lot of them raced at a professional level. But, I did become faster by trying to keep them in my sights. Many of them say I have a unique technique. I've also heard it said that you can see my skateboarding come through in my riding style. Being a skateboarder really helps your instincts when you need to eject your bike and roll out of a crash.

Crashing was something I was recognized for, the ability to not get too hurt and learning from the scrapes and burns transcended into knowing how to hit some pretty big jumps. At one point I had earned enough skill and confidence to hit a metal freestyle ramp which would launch its takers sky high.

Back to the track, I wanted to be a champion! So, I sandbagged. Sandbagging is a term racers use to describe someone who is knowingly faster than the class he enters. I entered the beginner/veteran class. I chose #70 for my race number, influenced by my space number #70 from the trailer park. I did win the championship, sandbagger as it was.

Still, it was not easy. I raced against some pretty fast men and I did not get 1st place every weekend. Showing up to every race and not going out with an injury was the key to my success. And, I did get to experience the unique rush that only a racer can relate too. This feeling of riding faster than your capabilities is called "riding over your head". Doing this slammed my body to the ground a few times. This is where my skateboarding wipe-out skills came into play, knowing when and how to abort a mission and put yourself in position to race another day.

During this one race at Glen Helen Raceway, I took a handle bar to the stomach. It felt like I got shot right in the middle of my upper abdomen. This took my breath away as it knocked the wind out of me, by now a familiar feeling.

When you almost wipe-out then regain control, it is often referred to as "Getting out of Shape". Funny because at the same time all this racing was getting me into shape. Because, unlike non-race situations, you're pushing yourself harder, faster and for longer. There is no time to stop and rest when you have a championship on the line.

Flow is often discussed when trying to explain the euphoric mixture between adrenaline and the power of being in the now. Athletes from all sorts of sports experience this state of extremely centered focus. It's like time stands still and your skills peak. Some of the best times of my life have been glimpses through this focused vision. That's what I see through the extreme sports lens. This is how I know flow.

As Darrin Hoeft and Damon Huffman were pulling into park at a riding spot, known as "Holley Land" (Jim Holley's place) in the desert, I overheard someone nearby say, "Those guys are Suzuki factory riders." Darrin pulled up to my truck, which had a sign airbrushed on the side "Water Wizards", my pool service. He introduced himself as a poolman also. So, hi and bye we met.

Less than a month later I was buying chlorine at the pool supply warehouse where Darrin's trail crossed mine again. We exchanged phone numbers and became the best of friends. Eventually geography and life pulled us apart the same way it brought us together, naturally. But, from October, 1991 through 2005 we talked every day. Those 15 years were the prime times when many of life's highlights took place.

We definitely had the same mindset, and career. Although, at the time he was attempting to make Moto-X his career. Darrin Hoeft was fast and famous enough to have his own Super-cross card. These cards were similar to baseball cards which also came with a stick of gum. On the backside of the cards they listed the racer's results from championships and other achievements.

Having Darrin as my every day friend really changed my life. His connections and friends were of the top names in the motocross industry. And through him I met all the top dogs on the scene in the 90's motocross era. We were bumping elbows with dozens of Moto-X stars on and off the track. Even drove in a car with Jeremy McGrath on one occasion and Ricky Carmichael gave me some of his hardly used boots. I was now a part of the scene. They had seen me through my "Vince's School of Moto-X" part in the "Throttle Junkies" video. Within a few years my name and photos were in magazines and on the cover of several video boxes. Riding with Darrin and Damon and the likes meant I would have to improve my riding skills. And, I did with their help and shared mindset. That was to do all we can as often as we could!

I wasn't the only one trying to keep up with this fast pack of riders. Scott McCormack, whom also is a poolman, was twisting the throttle pretty hard as well. Scott, Darrin and I all being our own bosses as poolmen never scheduled work for Mondays. We referred to this day of the week as "Poolman Meeting Mondays!" Religiously we would meet to have fun in the dirt. If it wasn't the dirt, then it would be snowboarding, surfing, wakeboarding or maybe some skateboarding. Either way we would seldom miss our ritualistic adrenaline packed meetings on Mondays.

After really prominent races, the top 3 places get on the podium where they have an opportunity to thank their sponsors publicly. Well, I've never been on the podium, but let me use this platform to thank Darrin Hoeft for the sponsorship/friendship. He was actually an accidental trainer to me, by making me a faster, stronger and a tougher rider. Thankful also for sponsoring me with gear, mostly hand-me-downs from his sponsored ware-robe. Damon Huffman also; these two guys gave me first hand help and tons of second hand stuff. They took me under their wings and literally taught me how to fly.

During this time period the top 4 bike brands were offering expert riders a cash/credit incentive to the top 3 riders in many races every weekend. This was referred to as Yamaha-dollars or Suzuki-bucks, something of that nature. But, you could only use this credit to purchase a new motorcycle as long as it was the same brand you were racing that day. Another stipulation was you needed to line up at the starting gate and race against at least 6 riders.

Well, one weekend there were only 5 experts that showed up to race. So, these 5 men were in need of someone to enter as an expert to fill the 6th spot. Lucky or unlucky, it turned out to be me to save their day. This time I was in the exact opposite position of sandbagging. Had I known I was going to race, swallowing those 4 Vicodin an hour earlier wouldn't have taken place. I was buzzing as I was contemplating. Nevertheless, I was committed. Some say that I should have been committed. That day I was wishing this novice had no vice.

The first lap I was desperately trying to keep up and as we hit the first big jump, I was only a few yards behind Darrin, but I was way out of shape. The front wheel was pointed straight up and it looked like I was going to loop out bad. I was feeling pretty loopy, figuratively and literally.

I hung onto the grips tighter than ever before and landed with the front wheel angled nearly at 12 o'clock. The impact jerked the handle bars out of one of my hands, but somehow I recovered. Darrin fell into the top 3 spots and collected his Suzuki bucks and all ended well that day.

Often our poolman Monday meetings turned into 18 hours days. We would wake up several hours before sunrise and drive 5 hours to Mammoth

Mountain to snowboard for 8 hours, then drive 5 hours back. Being a day-tripper can be exhausting. We played so hard that going back to work doing manual labor seemed relaxing.

Not everybody knows about this out-of-bounds location called "Hole in the Wall", but if you have been there you earned it. It starts by taking the chair lift to the highest point of Mammoth, then taking a hike to a drop in zone just past the Dragon's Back. From there you proceed to traverse until your legs are burning, then a little further.

The scenery and greenery are a delight splashed with white radiating – a pre-historic vibe, making you think maybe woolly mammoths might become un-extinct. It is so silent it makes your voice sound amplified. Your first time there should be with someone who has been there before. I had been guided there before with my Green Sector crew. With Darrin and Scott, I was the guide.

Upon arrival we rested with the relief that we didn't get lost. At first it looks like a cave, a cave big enough for a locomotive to drive into. But, when you position yourself to drop into this steep incline to enter the "hole in the wall", you can see that it is actually an organic tunnel. The already eerie feeling amplifies once you hear the echoing sound your snowboard makes as it shuffles the snow down in front of you.

Once you make it to the bottom and out the other side of the mountain, there is still more to the adventure. The "hole in the wall" is so far out-of-bounds that you need to take a bus back to the ski resort. And, the only way to the bus stop is to hike around a small lake, or across if it's frozen enough to support your weight. This always reminded me of the Jethro Tull lyrics "skating away on the thin ice of a new day".

I'm glad I was able to introduce Darrin to something new after all the new things he had introduced me to. It was a new day then, but it's an old day now.

It's safe to say that most people consider living a life primarily based on having fun is easy. Well, from my experience it is mentally but not physically.

The arms and legs are constantly being pushed and pulled and the lungs are often out of breath. The amount of G-force received would be unbearable without the help of the adrenaline which comes with the excitement. If you could bottle adrenaline, the sweat that was always involved would be one of the main ingredients.

As a poolman, if you start your job early and work at a rapid pace, you could finish by early afternoon. By then the arms could be pretty tired already, but we always seemed to find the energy to hook up the boat and cool off at the nearby Lake Castaic. The more you do something the better you get at it and that increases the amount of fun it can produce.

Darrin has been doing flips behind boats for decades and now into his 50's he still does. Wakeboarding is extremely physical and after some sessions, I would feel as if my arms were actually longer. Eat, sleep and clean swimming pools then back to Moto-x the next afternoon. I don't know if my arms were getting longer, but they were visibly getting bigger. Truth is nothing's easy. If you want to play, you have to pay. The price was a great investment because in the end you became a stronger man.

Many a weekend we would go to the Kings River with jet skis and many of our friends had boats. I could probably fill a hundred pages just talking about that place. But, the pages in this book are starting to add up, so I've selected to tell you about this rare occasion we had up in Central California at the Delta in exchange.

Darrin and I were behind two different boats deep in the Delta, being pulled side by side congruently. The two boats were so close together that only 50 feet behind them they had created a unique kind of wake where both boat wakes merged. So, Darrin and I collectively got creative and switched ropes and boats while cruising at 32 miles per hour. We took turns carving up this A-frame wave-like wake. Well, that's a very condensed version of the trip. Sorry, but I feel like I'm running out of rope and there is so much more I need to tie up.

Many of our adventures were documented, thanks to Scott McCormack and his video camera. Scott made one of the best 20 minute action sports videos I have ever been involved with. He edited it with great tunes and added some funny little skits of candid moments. It's titled "Friends". I do, and I believe my friends too, feel blessed to have had such an epic way of life for so long.

Skateboarding is one of the extreme activities that if you don't use it you lose it and the wipe-outs really hurt. Darrin, Scott and I still SK8. We went to skateparks in our 30's and we felt old then, but we were still pulling off hand plants and aerials on ramps 10' to 12' feet tall. We have skated a few times since then together at skateparks in pools and bowls. Personally, I find myself skateboarding more now in my 50's than I did throughout my 30's and the first half of my 40's. Those decades were filled with more extensive and expensive extreme sports.

Skateboarding is a convenient form of adrenaline infusion for me considering nowadays I live thousands of miles from the snow and from my friends with boats. Through adaptation I've re-adopted the alternative sport (anti-sport) of skateboarding. Another adrenaline rush I enjoy as an "aging but still raging" man is freestyling bicycle riding around town here in the tropical heat of Southeast Asia. I call it Manila Metro biking. The audience I have is never-ending. I'm constantly getting hoots and cheers (they often shout "one more" "tricks" and "stunts") from many of the 10 million people that populate this mega-city. I will do anything it takes to keep the adrenaline flowing and keep me in the flow-motion.

To sum it up, I miss my friends now that I am living on the other side of the planet. Oh well, nothing lasts forever and I feel that I am where I am supposed to be. I love being here with my wonderful wife, my dream girl. Fortunately I am a very vivid dreamer and I remember my dreams after awakening. Truthfully, a majority of my sleep is spent reminiscing those good old days. Sort of like an animated look at a history book with a twist from the future. Time traveling!

A huge part of being a motocrosser is being physically and mentally durable. Darrin Hoeft is that. He has paid and played through blood, sweat and tears. Moto-X has brought this man the most pleasure and the most pain anyone can acquire and endure!

In the early 90's at Super-x races when I heard the name Darrin Hoeft being announced through the loud speaker to over 50,000 people, I would think, "Man, these people are paying money to watch my friend ride a motorcycle". Then, later that decade with Damon Huffman I experience déjà vu as he went on to dominate super-cross. It was such a great deal and a big deal getting to ride regularly with them for free. Maybe they also felt it was time well spent as they seemed to be amused with my unique technique and enjoyed my company. A fortunate relationship is to be passionate about so many of the same things, priceless actually. I always felt the wealth of their friendship. Darrin is a lifer; he makes motorcycle riding seem like much more than . . . . . . anything.

Darrin married Michelle in the mid-90's and they're still going strong. Michelle is a teacher and very attractive; together they belong. And together they had two boys, Justin and Tyler. Justin Hoeft followed in his father's tire tracks racing Supercross. Super fast and full of prominent possibilities, currently making a lot of currency racing motorcycles. Darrin and his boys have done numerous photo shoots for dirt bike magazines. For decades Darrin has been an official test rider for Dirt Bike magazine and also does many photoshoots for Quad magazines. He has been displayed on many magazine covers and has stayed humble throughout this popularity.
It looked like his second son Tyler Hoeft was heading in the same direction as dad and big brother. Tyler was also super fast and just wildly exciting to be around. Even as a little kid, you would never know what to expect from Tyler. And, nobody could expect what was going to happen next.

We all know that there is a possibility, but we try not to think about it, as much as possible. Tyler was racing in Texas when the worst possible thing in life happened, death. Tyler's body slammed the face of a jump harder than living would allow. The impact killed him. He was helicoptered to the hospital from the track, but this was just a desperate effort to stop fate. He was only 14 years old, but being his dad's son provided him with more living life to the fullest moments than most will experience in a lifetime.

I was on the other side of the planet in the Philippines at the moment Tyler left this world to go into the great unknown. But, in that parallel moment, I had a mystical way of knowing something really bad had just happened to a best friend. Darrin's face just appeared in a waking thought. That morning before having coffee and checking my Facebook, Darrin's face with an "in shock" expression on it, stood suspended in front of me. Maybe it was a collective consciousness, some radio waves or a leaky wi-fi. But, I truthfully had a strong premonition that I was about to experience some bad news on social media that morning. An otherworldly telepathic communication is the closest I can come to explaining this unexplainable knowing.

Tyler's death occurred within the same two week time period as Heather's, Szabo's late wife. I felt terrible that my life was going so well at the time being freshly married to a fantastic wife, while two of my best friends were experiencing some of the greatest pains known to mankind. Both Tyler and Heather were present at my and Yolly's wedding. But, we couldn't even make it to their funerals. But no matter how terrible I felt, it was nothing in comparison to how Darren and Michelle or Szabo were going to feel for years to come.

Darrin contains a mental strength of the highest order, not to say that he is not very hurt. But a superman persona is prevalent when you're in his presence. He is one who is able to get back on that horse and ride. Coincidence or not he is a Sagittarius, which is the astrological symbol of a man that is part human part horse (half motorcycle). The media has often referred to the whole Hoeft family as having Moto-X in their blood. As for Michelle, well, her cousin is super-cross's legendary Damon Huffman and through him she met Darrin.

Many people may say "that's enough, sell the bikes". But, Darrin is not like many people. Justin went on and continued racing against other top professionals and does very well, except that he is often riddled with injuries. Through Moto-X this family has experienced the 4 basic emotions of being: Mad, glad, sad and scared to the fullest. And, as sure as the dust settled, through Moto-X we are from dust to dust. As the band Kansas put it, "All we are is dust to the wind".

Then and now, I wish words would help ease the pain. A pain that words can't even explain. Life's pleasures are spiked with pain, but we keep keeping-on just the same, riding this endless trail where we seamlessly find ourselves. Again and again, until ultimately there is no next time.

Normally Unusual Thoughts
N.U.T.
"The secret of genius is to carry the spirit of the child into old age, which means never losing your enthusiasm" – Aldous Huxley

The quote above had a strong spiritual impact on me, knowing the definition of enthusiasm is "being spiritually energized". This reminded me of Jesus's message that we need to return to a child-like innocence before returning to the Kingdom of God. I've often felt that we can live a life that relates to heaven on earth. Only problem is that heaven seems to be eternal and our time here on earth not so much. So, I often feel looking at pictures is a way for us to stop time.

Every life is an artwork, hence the word lifestyle. Your style of life with its own personal preferences. If we can master peace, we end up with a master piece, as we style our work.

I love to capture action shots of extreme sports. I find it to be an art form. I will admit it. I have a normally unusual amount of pictures of myself caught in the act of action. And, I'm sure to some people I appear vain. For me this just might be a vain attempt to live forever, or maybe it is something I just enjoy without a need for explanation.

To be able to record an ability of which I possess, an ability I may no longer have in the future, is an option I have always taken. To relive that moment in time is worth the price I pay. In my time of calendar youth the price was high, paying for the film and then again being charged for the developing got very expensive.

Nowadays in my still active youthful old age, the cost is free. The digital world is wonderful. Currently most of my action pictures are (selfies) that I take with video from a phone camera, which I position in an artistic location. While resting and recuperating from the photo'd stunt, I view the footage in slow-motion. The next step is to press the pause button at the peak performance second then snap a screen shot. I follow up with editing the color, texture and lighting, then hit "save". By hitting a couple more buttons, the photo is instantaneously sent around the globe via social media. It's like presto, whallah, a magic also known as wi-fi. I can do all of this for free and often even before my sweat even dries. To stay in the flow created by motion. Hocus-pocus, I re-focus and do it again. Never running out of film to bring it to an end . . . . and do it again!

Studying pictures of your action sports can help you improve your style and technique. Moto-X racers often review footage of their races between motos, making them faster as a result. In pause or slow-motion we can see things that the human eye cannot, another-worldly view, if you will.

Aging and forgetfulness are inevitable, but pictures provide instant memory, allowing us to relive flashbacks of our always younger appearance.

Through the imagination of technology, we are now allowed to look into the future with photo projection imagery. This application started out as just a dream or I could say a ""justavision" to see an older version of ourselves.

At night when I dream I see pictures no one has seen, always a new scene in my imagination. The contents of my dreams are often influenced by thoughts of who or what I'm writing about. I have experienced this during the making of this book, a sort of sleep script, and of course nothing goes as planned. Our daily experiences set the dreamscape. Then it's an impromptu act from there. As we simultaneously become both the actor and the audience.

I enjoy my sleep life almost as much as my waking life, mainly because gravity does not always exist, yet sometimes I'm weighed down by some heavy emotions. As I float and fly about, the possibilities are endless.

Every picture tells a story of fact and fiction, as different people always see a different thing (within) the same picture. As a picture paints a thousand words, each reader translates the story the way they see it. A view that is true for them.

By stretching the imagination, we can picture that one day there may be an instrument that can record our dreams and develop photos of the inside of our minds - similar to a CT scan. If this image develops, would it make you photogenic or give you a photographic memory? This is another normally unusual thought that I have had. And, I imagine I'm not the only one.

Life is a long song, but the tune ends too soon for most people's liking. So, we record it in hopes of replaying it again and again, time after time. Taking pictures is similar to recording songs. Songs and pictures conjure up emotions which we replay/relive. By writing each chapter as a song, I've somewhat seen my book as an album. I also see the writer and the musician both as artists, as well as the photographer.

Photography brings forth emotion, an emotion we clutch to even tighter when the photos become ghost cards. Pictures of our late loved ones who cannot be photographed anymore have extreme potential at bringing forth heavy emotions. I look at these (ghost cards) with feelings that have been transported from immeasurable distances. We may feel mad, glad, sad and fearful all within one glance of these photos of those we have lost.

I've heard talk of a smell-a-vision app, but find this only imaginable. Some say that if it can be imagined, then it is just a matter of time before it is manufactured, in a sense matured to fact. I believe imagination exceeds reality. There are some things that are just impossible. Period. It would be crazy (unreasonable), right? Smell-a-vision.

Dreams provide an arena for the imagination to exceed what is possible in the waking life. In life everything changes, growth and aging are undeniable. Change normally involves some pain, hence "life is painful". Only in pictures change is denied, the captured moment continues unchanged. A form of time travel, both pictures and dreams provide.

A major percent of people spend a major percent of time looking at pictures. From moving pictures on the big screen and everything in between to social media which is based on pictures. More life, more friends and more time, times of our life that have been captured, contained and condensed into obtainable content, to our hearts content. As we process and digest this material we do both give and receive. This is also the nature of time.

For most identity begins as a picture taken from our mama's bellies, though we don't remember that experience. This leads me to believe that even though we don't have photos of the afterlife yet, in time we have an afterlife experience. Given that, it is not necessary to be identified to exist.

Memory comes and goes, but existence is eternal. Even if you can't picture it. And, though this seems impossible to understand, understanding is not a requirement to receive this experience. The image of an afterlife may go beyond our imaginations. And I pray that a conclusion is just an illusion.

CHAPTER 7

"ALL WASHED UP"

"Is it better to burnout or fade away?"

As the waters were rising "I K.W.I.T." was about to be all washed up. Living on the river bed front property gave way to a beautiful daily view, but also gave way to seasonal flooding. This allowed me many years of adventures for river rafting right out my front door.

I would like to go into more depth about two adventures I've had floating down the Santa Clarita riverbed, both involved helicopters and rushing waters. Also, there was the one dark night I fished my black lab (Moto) out of the deep strong current too swift for dog paddling. But, I must back paddle the pen to keep up with the flow of this story before this book becomes too flooded with words.

Country living in Canyon Country, California allowed me to live in the great outdoors. Some say "the "Great Out Doors" is an acronym for G.O.D. This atmosphere made me imagine cowboys had once ridden horses here. On occasion, I would shoot my .22 caliber rifle right off the front porch. Of course, I would only do this while drinking alcohol, being not a very sober thing to do. There was the school house and many resided within a bullet's distance from my noisy and hazardous target practice. This is more proof that I have gotten away with more than I should have during my years of living like an outlaw, in God's country.

History has it that the Sand Canyon Mobile Home Park was built on ancient Indian trading grounds. If this location was a sound, it would be the sound of Country Western music, but from 1992 through 2004. The ground here felt the vibrations of the extremely loud music of I KWIT.

Less than a quarter mile downstream from my house perched up on a hilltop set an ancient burial ground (graveyard). There you can find the Mitchell family is buried. Legend has it that they had bought or traded the land from the Indians to build the Sand Canyon Mobile Park. The tombstones bear their names along with many others, but some tombstones had no names, only descriptions such as Mexican Baby or Daughter. These are very vivid memories buried in the archives of my mind. And soon my house would be buried nearby.

During this time period, I was freshly sober again. Similar to the incident in 1994 when my first mobile home had fallen to the ground during that groundbreaking earthquake. Sober enough to really feel tragedy shake me up! And, this was about to shake me up as well as soak me down.

Heavy rain had been soaking the ground for two weeks solid now. My girlfriend and I were looking out the window from my home (Space #70). The flowing water was growing as the space between my house was going. And, as it was shrinking, I was thinking, "Man, I better not start drinking."

She was a wonderful girlfriend, eleven years younger than myself. Together our energy multiplied. She used some of this energy to help me clean my 56 swimming pools every week and on the weekends I would introduce her to some normally unusual experiences in the great outdoors. It was great to work with a companion; being a poolman is a lonely career. I was really starting to fall for her. And, I wasn't the only thing about to fall.

We were feeling anxious watching the river swell. So, we decided to distract our minds by watching a movie. In the theater watching "Meet the Fockers", my mind was far from the imminent danger of losing the house I truly loved, when my cell phone rang. It was Lump, my roommate, with the suggestion that I return home as soon as possible. This was a hard movie to walk away from, but his voice had the tone of pertinence.

Within 5 minutes of our arrival, we started evacuation procedures. The river was already peeling back the chain-link fence like the lid of a canned good. Evacuation I was familiar with for it was my 3rd experience at Space #70 doing so. First, after the 1994 earthquake. Then again, in 1998 when a flood took a section of my yard with the mud.

Always my neighbors were so helpful, backing truck after truck into my driveway to help load up many of my belongings. Time was getting shorter by the minute to an unknown conclusion. As it was also getting dark, I had to decide on which I might have to say good bye to. My pool table and piano stayed behind.

My two dogs at the time had always been a great emotional support to me and me to them. There was so much anxiety and stress that evening. I felt the three of us had this special connection. The looks in their eyes spoke a 1,000 words. I took them to the swimming pool area and locked the gate unknowing of what would become our fate.

Obviously too dangerous to sleep in my house that night as the rain remained a constant curtain. The river was creeping up slowly but surely as it was erasing big chunks of my real estate. While watching the land disappear, we decided to spend the night at my girlfriend's house in Sylmar about 20 minutes away.

Pretty much a sleepless night, my perception of time was lost as the consistent pounding of the rain on the roof turned the sound of every water drop into the ticking of a time clock. Actually for years after that night when I heard the tapping of rain, it often sounded like the tick, tick, ticking of a time bomb!

Earlier that afternoon I was standing on the edge of understanding that P.T.S.D. does not stand for Post Traumatic Surfer Disorder. Also standing on the edge of the rapidly moving rapids of the river was my skateboard half-pipe ramp. My ramp was 16 feet wide and 4 feet of it was hanging over the deep dark water. My friend, Paul, was there with his video camera and shouts out, "Vince, take the last skate run on the ramp before it's all washed up."

Skateboarding is similar to surfing, but with skating you usually are dry. But, this was a normally unusual circumstance. So, I took a stance on my board and from the top of the ramp I dropped in! Rain pouring down with all the wet giving my ramp the simulation of a wave crashing down. Within 5 minutes after surfing my skateboard ramp, it had fallen into the great flush of the flooding tide, never to be seen again, except on film.

The tree which I had built a treehouse in was next to go. And, then the garage shed where we had just evacuated my motorcycles. The shed hit the water when the land slid from beneath. The unforgettable noise sounded like a tool box being shook up. All my tools, wrenches, nuts and bolts were still inside. The shed left my property with a smack, rattle and pop! It did not sink; it just floated away in one piece to a not too peaceful demise.

By now there were half a dozen news media vans and cameras rolling in front of my house. Several of them wanting to interview me on the spot. And, on the spot, I rambled off part of my rap from the one you read in the beginning of this book, "Then, Happened, Now". It was televised and ended up being viewed all over the world. This was a pretty big event, but most of the news shifted to the La Conchita land slide that had claimed many lives that same day.

By the time nightfall had darkened the scene, my house was suspending over the edge of the river. After that restless night, we returned to Space #70 early the next morning to find my home teeter tottering on the edge between land and water. Lump's room was dangerously dangling in peril and the whole house was in jeopardy!

The T.V. cameras were filming and I had a microphone stuck in front of my face again as they asked for answers to their questions. And, right in between my words I heard a terrible creaking, almost a screeching sounds. Upon turning, I saw the vision of my home splashing as it was crashing into the river.

A strange sense of relief overtook me. I was no longer in suspense.

It was like I was on a unique adrenaline high. Waiting ahead of me the true meaning of P.T.S.D. I would understand as Post Traumatic Stress Disorder. Something had changed. Shit, everything had changed.

A week or so later while cleaning pools I looked up and saw the clouds as I never had seen them before. They held more meaning, too much meaning. Then, while riding my motorcycle in the mountains with Lump, we rode across a shallow stream and the water appeared to me to be a material. This was a hallucination type of vision but not in a good way. More like a bad acid trip, if that makes sense. Something about (water) – an element that is both harmless and hazardous at the same time.

What did not make sense was that I was riding dirt bikes with my friend and it didn't seem like fun. Usually it's a blast, normally. I've learned since then that what was happening was an anxiety attack, one of many to come throughout the next 10 years.

I told Lump I wasn't feeling right and I would have to leave immediately. There was a highway nearby that would take me to the campsite where I was now living. The highway was illegal for dirt bikes, but I didn't care. I needed to get home, fast! This experience now leads me to believe it may have been a precursor to agoraphobia as well. Though, I can never stay inside too long, sometimes it has felt very hard to leave a home.

Anxiety is not a sign of weakness, but rather a sign that you have been too strong for too long. Sometimes having a strong imagination can become a heavy burden when we realize that we cannot control all of our thoughts all of the time. Basically, I had started to worry that I worried too much about worrying.

Back then some sounds like a certain pop when they hit my ears would trigger thoughts of my house hitting the water. Right after the house hit the water, it began sinking. The air trapped inside the house was looking for a way out. Finally, "pop" the air pressure burst through Lump's bedroom window. As the window popped out, it instantly became the escape hatch for all of his floatable belongings.

It was almost comical watching our valuables rise to the top and drift out of sight, at the same damn time, knowing they were heading toward the ocean. But, there was nothing really funny about it. The laughs were not hysterical, but hysterics, a release of tension similar to the broken glass that availed the vision. Similarly when my anxiety gets too high, I often throw up. Getting sick is a way for the tension to release. I would feel like I was going to self-implode.

Before the flood I had it all, materially speaking. I owned my own home and business, had 3 motorcycles, drove a brand new Toyota truck and the list goes on. Too much material stuff to mention and at this time I also had a good looking girlfriend that was only in her 27th year. But, by the end of that day I could fit everything I owned into the back of my truck. Oh well, at least I had a pretty girl sitting in the passenger seat. Well, at least for a few more weeks.

The future was uncertain and the end was here. The end of living in my dream home. Dreams can turn into nightmares fairly fast. She cancelled all the plans, hopes and dreams we had made together. One word she used while breaking up with my heart was "overwhelming". She had said that I was overwhelming. I had to agree. I was overwhelmed by the world my life reflected.

I took the break up way too hard. My emotions by this point were already exaggerated, beyond balance. I couldn't take it anymore. I needed a potion to control my emotion. So, I started drinking and drugging again. I had lost all hope and I didn't know how to cope without dope. At the time I just couldn't see how I would ever be able to be living the dream again.

Right after the submersion of my house, I bought a brand new 2005 American Pride 23 foot camper trailer – an instant new home. All I needed was a place to park it. I was lucky enough to find a place high in the mountains of Acton. And similar to the time 18 years prior when I lived camping in Acton, this also was on 5 acres, also up two dirt roads.

My new home for the next 2 years was rather dreamy. The land I rented to park and live provided water, electricity and sewage, so I was set. The location was so far from a highway that the sounds of silence were surreal. The wind would carry the breath of the leaves away as I listened to the trees breathe. The vista could take your breath away as well.

I was able to continue riding dirt bikes from home. This location provided hundreds of new trails for exploration. The mountain range was gigantic, an enormous vast place where echoes exist, for my Moto-X crew to explore new uncharted terrain (terra firma). This opened the door to a whole new collection of adventures.

Losing so many of my possessions to the flood was difficult, but I was reimbursed by the state and the insurance company and ended up with close to $100,000. I made investments immediately by buying 2 jet skis and then 2 dune buggies. Even after being shaken-up and soaked-up by earthquakes and floods, I continued my thirst for adrenaline fixations. And, these new high-dollared and high-powered toys were to be my new tools to continue playing a life focused on fun.

I continued my thirst for alcohol as well. Living life off the wagon and having a seemingly endless beer budget, both would burn themselves out as I watched them fade away. Many of my desires proved to be dangerous. Still having the mind of an addict, I started to desire taking another psychedelic trip, a vacation from reality and even from myself. This turned out to be an outer body experience.

Salvia is a hallucinogen strong enough to produce astral projection. The street name for this drug is "Sally Space". So, I am smoking it through my bong intending to take three hits. I finished two hits and then left my body and got up and walked to the couch from the table in my trailer. I sat down on the couch and watched myself finish the third hit while the other me was sitting at the table smoking it. I'm not lying; there were two of me and to this day, I can't tell you which one was the real me.

As I'm watching myself, this Indian steps into my trailer with feathers on his head, a knife on his side and moccasins on his feet. He turned to talk and the vibrations of his voice caused my camper trailer to grow and double in size. Then he looked into my eyes and said to me while pointing to the other me, "Man! That guy is going to be sooooo out of his mind." I heard this as I was out of my body.

So, I'm like "Whatever dude; I gotta get out of here." I walked past the Indian and out my door into the outside world, while leaving the other me inside the trailer to talk to the Indian. I wanted to stay and hear what they had to discuss, but I was feeling claustrophobic even though my home had become twice the size it was just moments earlier.

Walking outside, I started to feel a very uncomfortable tingling and twitching of my body. A very hot and itchy feeling stayed with me for a short time. And, then I snapped out of it and found myself outside. As I write this and think about it, I realize I must have been the one that walked away and left myself behind. Either way, it was a very strong and vivid outer body experience. Some people would consider this a near death experience. It definitely had some of the same elements.

Around the corner awaited another near death experience or I should say at the top of the mountain. This time no drugs or alcohol were involved. Still, I truly believe I came close to the edge. I was on a solo mission just cruising my dune buggy through the dirt. From the top, I started descending down a very steep and potentially ominous mountain. It was so steep that I knew applying the brakes the whole way down would be necessary to refrain the momentum from getting beyond my control. I soon found out that using the brakes was useless; they were non-existent. Total and complete brake failure. The brakes had broken. I tried pumping the brake pedal which in some cases works, but as I was doing this, my speed was gaining rapidly.

After losing all hope in my feet getting me out of this, I turned my attention to my hands by attempting to steer my way out of this mess. And as I was trying to traverse this 45 degree angle, I realized I was heading toward the steeper of the two options. To the right was certain death. To the left, left me with better odds. Well, as I was completing the 2nd S-turn, gravity turned me towards my fate. I was processing the situation as if it were in slow motion. As I felt and saw the wheels rising fast from the ground over my head, I relocated my hands from the steering wheel to the top roll-bar above my upside down head.

My seatbelt was on, but this new-to-me buggy had probably 20 years of fun and sun on it already. Luckily, the brittle, sun-scorched seatbelts kept me in, or maybe it would have been better to have been thrown out. At this point, I would have preferred an ejection seat and a parachute!

So, as it was, my hands were caught between the earth and the top of the dune buggy being smashed and crushed by the impact of gravity. And this was the 1st of 3 revolutions end over end. Feeling the pressure, but not the pain yet, I pulled my hands in toward my body and relied on the seat belts for the next two revolutions. The 3rd roll seemed like I was in the air for a long time. This was because I had now fallen off a 20 foot cliff straight onto flat ground. The buggy and I just laid there like a turtle on his back.

My first thought was "Cool, I'm still alive". My second thought was "Oh, no, this buggy might catch fire and blow up". Gas was already leaking from the upside down gas tank. I noticed blood dripping from my glove, but I would take care of the problem at hand first. First thing I needed to do was to get the four wheels on the dirt again.

I have heard many stories about people having superhuman strength when high levels of adrenaline were involved. Usually stories of a parent lifting a car off their child when one was trapped underneath. Well, I've never had kids, but I believe I had experienced this superhuman strength. Within minutes, I had that dune buggy from upside down to right side up!

I felt extremely charged up at that moment. The adrenaline had somehow electrically charged every cell in my body. Remarkably and almost unbelievably, the buggy actually started back up. I drove it slowly back to my camper less than a mile away. The buggy was all bent up with multiple broken parts and barely made it back to my camp. Surprisingly, it was doing more of the limping that I was.

About an hour later I was notably tired and fatigued, probably from being stronger than humanly possible. By exerting the energy to lift this buggy to its wheels, I went from being superhuman to being super depleted. Energy was dying; every cell in my body was burnt out. I felt like I had been close to the edge and even a little further. I also felt lucky to be alive. And, with my dyslexic twist, I also felt alive to be lucky!

I love both my parents as much as life itself, as much as my life itself could not exist without the love they share. Regardless of this strong love I have for them, I was still incapable of contacting them both on days of celebration for parents. My first failed connection happened on Mother's Day. A day I was so drunk from morning to night that I couldn't even make a phone call.

The next day I was full of remorse and also full of alcohol poisoning. In the hospital with saline solution being pumped into my veins was actually preferable to the extreme pain that filled my eyes outside. Everything seemed too bright that day, except me.

Then came Father's Day, which was a trip because of all these "clear as day" coincidences. Such was that day I went jet skiing with a friend whose father had recently died from a heart attack. We were heading to the ocean from Acton when my fatherless friend gave me some pills of which I can't even remember what they were. We were pretty dizzy and messed up by the time we were in the ocean.

We headed south a few miles from Ventura Harbor on the jet skis to ride the waves at Oxnard Shores. I wiped out while riding on a really big wave, probably due to my drug altered balance. My jet ski tumbled and flooded to the point where it would not start again.

Being a strong swimmer, I was able to pull the jet ski far enough out to sea to keep it from getting washed up on shore. The currents were strong that day, so every 10 minutes I would have to pull the jet ski by swimming west. My friend was there to help, but it was hopeless because we were ropeless. So, my friend headed back to Ventura Harbor to find a tow rope while I waited.

They say it's a small world and at times I've had to say it's a small ocean. I looked to the south and saw a jet ski from a distance heading north towards me. Instantly I hoped this guy had a tow rope so I could hitch a ride. As he got close enough to identify, I realized he was one of my neighbors from Acton, coincidentally. But, the strange coincidence taking place on this Father's Day was that he had a son who had just died. So, this sonless father friend of mine hooks me up with his tow rope and starts towing me back to the harbor.

While entering the harbor, we idled up to a huge National Coast Guard vessel on a search and rescue mission heading out to sea looking for a person fitting my description. Well, it was me they were looking for. I guess my pill popping fatherless friend found the Coast Guard before he could find a rope. I shouted up from the water that their search was over and sorry for the inconvenience.

It was my intention to visit my Dad in San Fernando Valley for Father's Day on the way back to Acton. But, by then I was way too wasted from the beers we were drinking while driving. So, I just kept driving with my head hung low past my parent's house.

I knew I was at risk of getting put in jail for drunk driving, so I took the back streets and alley ways all the way back to Acton. This doubled the travel time and I was having double vision as well, but I could still see this would cut my risk of getting caught in half. The next morning my truck and jet ski trailer had dents, broken tail lights and many scratches, none of which I can recall. I had reached a black out drunk experience, another one of many.

Having me as a son would be tough. I was blessed to have come from a set of super strong parents. And, of course, I am extremely sorry for all the grievances I have caused. If I outlive my parents, I will be consoled at the time of their passing knowing that I saved them from the pain of my death, as things are easier to accept in a chronological order. I know my numerous close calls have been a burden, but I believe they know that I would never intentionally hurt them. The problem with drugs and alcohol is that things never go the way you intentionally want them to. Through the A.A. program, we learn how to make an amends and this amends depends upon the continuation of our sobriety. I have also learned how selfish I can be even when that's not my intention.

I had several other close calls on those two jet skis as well. I would often take them to the ocean and ride the waves, to the river riding the currents sometimes even the rapids, but most often it was the lakes. My arms were getting really big from the tricks I was learning on these high powered watercraft, but while they were getting bigger my wallet was getting smaller. The trips and gas were burning up a lot of money.

By 2006, half my pool route (27 pools) had sold to a Russian. This left me with so much time to jet ski, now only working two days a week. About 9 months later, I sold the remaining pools to an El Salvadorian. It is interesting to see the world's population getting all mixed up. My curiosity again started to wonder what it would be like to live in another country.

Neither of the next two countries I chose to live in produced snow in their mountains. Up until 2006, snowboarding had stayed a consistent part of my life. As my days of snowboarding were melting, I went out with a last snow memory as a snowboard instructor at Mtn. High. Each day I would teach the youth of America how to excel in what I considered an art form - an art form that was not even around when I was their age. The freezing cold mornings at Mtn. High would be the last times I had experienced the pain of numb and frozen body parts. It was a lasting memory that I would often reflect back to at times of near heat stroke that came to my future of living in tropical heat.

My good friend, Don Szabo, was planning a surf trip to Costa Rica with 6 of his friends in February of 2006, so I said, "Count me in!" The trip was supposed to be for one week. And it was, for everyone but me. I loved the place so much that I stayed for an additional week on my own solo surf safari. Being alone in a strange country was a feeling I would come to know well, as my future would cross a few more borders along my sometimes lonely journey.

That 1st week we had surfed on the Pacific Ocean side of the country. The 2nd week I wanted to see what the Caribbean side was like. I've heard it was called the dark side. Partly because that side has been known to be dangerously sketchy. Partly also because a lot of Jamaicans were shipped over to help build a railroad. As a result, a lot of Costa Ricans on that side have darker skin.

While surfing in 3rd world countries, I have found the police to take my money, rather than the bad guys. A couple of times in Mexico and now in here Costa Rica, 3 times in a 24-hour period.

Before my trip to the dark side, I found myself further south than I had ever been. I was in a bar looking up at a big screen TV and to my surprise I also found myself on that TV screen. This bar in Jaco, Costa Rica was the sports bar type, the extreme sports type. They were playing one of the action videos I had ridden dirt bikes in. So, in a sense, I was there before I was there. After a few more beers and a burrito, I got on the road, just me and my surfboard wide open along with a bottle of rum, speeding along the highway with a good buzz not knowing a police car was following me. I looked in the mirror to find my 2nd surprise that day so far.

I had enough colones (Costa Rican money) on me to know that this would just be an expense and a delay. But, still there was a possibility of being arrested for driving under the influence. The big smile of a female policia with a Jamaican accent greeted me and the bribe went pleasantly, only costing me $60 US Dollars. Her accent made me feel like I was getting near my destination.

I would soon find a motel right on the Caribbean water. And, after a little swim in an ocean new to me, it became dark on a moonless night.

In America you never see two policemen on one motorcycle, but it is very common in the underdeveloped world. It looked funny to me when they pulled up behind me, but these two would have the last laugh. I was smoking pot sitting on a log close to the water. But, not close enough to the water to throw my marijuana that far. It was very dark, but they had flashlights and guns of which they pulled out. They found my pot and kept it. So, I figured, "OK, fine you can have it." But, they wanted more than that, they wanted money, $200 US Dollars to be exact. But, I was short due to the $60 I had used as a "get out of jail" card earlier.

My room was in sight, so I pointed to it and said, "My money is up there. Can I please get my wallet? I promise I will come back." Maybe the policia were thinking I might not return, so they took my picture and said that if I did not return, they would find me and shoot me. So, after my photo opportunity, I went to my room, but honestly didn't have $200 for my ransom. What I did have was Szabo's i-Pod he had lent me. i-Pods had just recently been invented and he said, "Don't lose it; it cost $300." But, it was all I had to offer up as a bribe, being I didn't think they would be interested in my surfboard, nor did I want to let that go.

So, I returned to the scene and they looked as nervous as I felt. They kept looking around, not wanting anyone to see them in the middle of their extortion. They quickly accepted my bail and left me without any pot and now tuneless as well.

Waking up the next day not to the sound of music, but to the sound of my addiction telling me to find more pot. I still had enough money to score, but no connections to hook up some dope. So, I bought another bottle of rum instead. Strange how the most dangerous drug (alcohol) is legal worldwide.

I decided I loved the Costa Rican Pacific side, but I don't even like this side of the country. So, I got breakfast, then broke out of town rapido. And, as I'm driving back to the side I love, I'm taking a few hits of rum to take the edge off. When you're an addict, you don't see drugs and alcohol as the problem. The problem is how you see life without them. So, you always want to be under the influence of something. Normally I preferred marijuana until noon, then marijuana and alcohol 'til midnight.

Driving away from the dark side having mixed feelings, feeling lucky and unlucky simultaneously, I was also feeling the effect of the rum starting to numb my head. Speeding along the same stretch of road where I got pulled over the day before I got pulled over again, now going the opposite direction. I was in the same condition, drunk.

Being more of a fast driver than a fast learner, I told the policia hombre that it was $60 US yesterday and that I was having a déjà vu. I don't know if he understood English, but money seems to be the universal language.

My next (look for a new place to live) mission was Hawaii. Szabo spent the 2nd week exploring the place with me. I had arrived a week earlier. The 1st week in Hawaii I was on an economic solo surf safari. Saving money on motel rooms by sleeping in my rental car, which was a Jeep Cherokee. The nights were miserable, but the days refreshing. Occasionally in the middle of the night I would wake up from the heat and run the motor so I could have temporary A.C. The hot humid windless nights paid off with sweet clear warm water waves. Also enjoyable was a long hike through the rainforest, barefoot and shirtless filled with deep thoughts.

Szabo was going to meet me on the Big Island of Hawaii where he had a friend who would let us spend a week at his house in Kona. It was the night before I was supposed to pick Szabo up at the airport when I found a place to park and sleep. It was so dark and I was so drunk that I didn't realize where I had parked. I awoke surprised at how close I was to the water. Literally 20 feet from the Pacific Ocean with my 4 x 4 wheel drive tires set up upon lava rock. As I focused my eyes, I could see the Captain Cook monument statue on the other side of the bay, maybe a ¼ mile away.

After I processed where I was, I opened the back hatch of the Jeep Cherokee which was facing the water. I started to pee using my left hand as I usually do. Then, the earth started shaking fiercely. The earthquake caused the huge cliff that ran across the entire bay to fall 300 feet to the ocean. As if God himself had chiseled a 20 foot thick chunk of vertical mountain roughly a ¼ mile wide and chopped it down with the edge of His hand.

I grabbed my camera with my free right hand and as I was still peeing I snapped some incredible pictures of this huge piece of earth disappearing into the ocean. The water displacement was so extreme that it caused a reverse tsunami, a 4 foot wave rolled out away from the cliff and into the deep blue sea leaving behind a light brown sky. Seeming stranger than fiction, I found it unreal and surreal at the same time.

There were several mid-sized boats anchored pretty close to the impact zone. The dust produced by this explosion of earth consumed visibility of these vessels. In the air was the sound of two girls screaming hysterically "Grampa . . . . Grampa!!"

I walked over to see what was going on. They said, "Our Grandpa is on that boat." I said, "Get in my Jeep. I will drive you two closer to him."

After I dropped them off, the next thing I can remember was trying to find the local newspaper headquarters so I could submit my "sure to be" front page photos.

On my arrival at the corner of the building appeared another strange and rare photo opportunity. It was a mongoose and a cat each hidden to the view of the other by the 90 degree corner of the building. One was aware of the other, but I can't remember which was the hunter or which was being hunted.

So, along with that picture and the cliff falling into the sea photos, I entered the building. The place was thrashed. All their equipment was on the floor broken and still no electricity. The staff was bewildered and shaken from the quake. And, sadly, they were unable to download my photos.

All this had taken place while Szabo was suspended in the air on his flight which was due to land in a couple of hours. First thing he said at the airport was "Vince, you seem to be magnetic towards disaster." I had to agree. I always seem to be in the wrong place at the right time, or dyslexically in the right place at the wrong time.

Yin and Yang are a dualism concept based on seemingly opposites or contrary forces which may be interconnected. I have always felt connected to the lyrics "good times, bad times, you know I've had my share."

From California, I thought of moving over 1,000 miles north to Canada, then pondered on moving 2,500 west to Hawaii. But, by 2007 I ended up moving 3,800 miles to Costa Rica. And, now 2 decades into the 3rd millennium A.D. I'm living and writing this from so far west over the horizon that it actually turned into the far east, over 7,000 miles away from my point of origin. As a result, I have passed through the international timeline to reside in the Philippines here in Southeast Asia and I feel like a traveler of both time and space. As times of our futures past are waiting for us, we are left behind, by moving forward.

"Normally Unusual Thoughts"
N.U.T.

"Remain sane, refrain brain strain"

Life can be simply complicated. Everybody wants to be happy and many think they will be when they get what they want. Switch it up, wanting what you get brings happiness. Seldom, the other way around. The complicated part that is not so simple to understand is that unhappiness produces irritation, anxiety, depression and the fear that we may never be happy again. This became clear to me when I experienced the loss of my home, my happy place.

People can resent more than just other people, such as places and events. Admittedly or not, I had a resentment about losing my planned future at the Sand Canyon Mobile Home Park of which I had worked so hard to obtain. Since then I have owned up to my past, while learning that the future is something that can never be owned.

As an alcoholic I cannot afford the luxury of having resentments. Non-alcoholics may find resentments to be problematic, but not necessarily deadly. Resentments are the #1 cause of relapse amongst alcoholics; it's a real killer. Today I'm glad I can't afford resentments, seeing now that they hold little to no value.

In the program of A.A. we learn not to play the blame game, finding shame and guilt to be something that should not be delegated. Though it's natural for people to blame when they feel powerless. Whether it is a person, place or thing that we resent, we need to own up to our part in the situation. We can do this by asking ourselves what is our part in the matter. Where are we being (1) dishonest (2) self-centered (3) resentful (4) fearful, I use this method often for quick relief. Some other effective tools we use are acronyms, for example: H.O.W. Honesty, Open mindedness, Willingness. Somethings are worth repeating and you may hear a similar paragraph in the chapter devoted solely to recovery. In the meetings, principles are often repeated and that is helpful as we seem to be forgetful.

Of course alcoholics don't have a monopoly on living without resentments. It's just that we find resentments to be life threatening. Al-Anon also applies these same tools and techniques, managing to achieve happiness as well. These and all 12-Step programs are spiritual solutions to problems that occur in this material world. If the whole world used this spiritual program, no wars would ever be started due to disagreements. These 12 suggestions would make a responsible population incapable of blaming others. Deflating egos would create World peace.

Regardless of which religion you chose or inherited, these steps can work for you to live a life free from resentments. A religion is a deal where if you follow the rules you get rewarded; you break the rules you get punished. Spirituality is a journey where you continue to grow towards enlightenment. Enlightenment to me is about unlearning the fictitious reality which has shaped our history with the usage of stories that we are expected to believe. Often the people that did not go along with the story were labeled crazy and shamed. This might be why history seems to be repeating itself. Luckily as the human race evolves, less and less people are believing everything they are told. The answers are found in the questioning.

What I mean by fictitious reality is best explained through the comparisons between us and the animal kingdom. This is another highly believed story where we set ourselves up to be superior, them inferior. The difference between our four-legged friends and us are the layers of reality we recognize. The animals recognize two realities, subjective and objective. (1) What they see externally (objective) and (2) what their interpretation of it is (subjective). Humans have this as well, but we also observe a 3rd layer of reality (the inter-subjective) which by definition means a collective belief.

When almost everyone believes in the same thing, it makes it convincing that this is just how it is, a forced reality.

"A lie told a thousand times becomes a truth."

Usually society will label you insane if you don't believe in the story. Examples of this could be borders, governments, superstitions and traditions of which are mental constructs, a consensual hallucination of the collective consciousness. These stories are what make us human. It goes without saying that our complex language skills set us apart from our furry friends, as well. Animals can't relay stories, nor misinterpret them. So, false beliefs can't be carried from generation to generation. With animals, there are no deviations between generations.

The plus side to our intrinsic and detailed form of communication, which animals don't have, allows us to build technology and enormous cities and cars. Our opposable thumbs help a lot as well!

All of these social constructs that we are supposed to live up to create a lot of expectations, which when unmet lead to anxiety, depression and agitation. In some cases one may even feel self-resentment for going along with these stories that we inherited, instead of rewriting their beliefs through their own experiences. Humans are very efficient at adapting to the abnormal until it seems normal. Protocols get set in place and stay there long past any logical reasoning exist.

As the rain moves the mountains and the clouds move the rain, I take a deep breath and remain sane, refrain brain strain and endure the pain. I've found happiness through the loving of life, but first I had to forgive life itself. After all there is no resentment where forgiveness is found.

CHAPTER 8

"PSYCHEDELIC SURF SEDUCTION"

"Today was different . . . . "

Everything looked, tasted and smelled different. This, my new life, feeling far from the same. Everything had changed. Living in Costa Rica, finding a place to get lost in time. The time was 40 days before Easter 2007 as the plane landed in Central America on Ash Wednesday. Growing up Catholic I always practiced Lent, 40 days and 40 nights of sacrifice, as a sort of repentance for my sins in the honor of the resurrection of Jesus on Easter.

Ever since I was 15 years old I would attempt to stop drinking beer and smoking pot for this time period. Sometimes I succeeded, but usually not. Not innocent, but in a sense I was practicing recovery since the beginning of my using. Nevertheless, relapse was included in my pre-meditation. Lent, to me, was similar to a New Year's resolution and about 40 days and nights seemed more doable than a whole year. No matter what stretch of abstinence you are in, a day is a day, some doable and some undoable. Since then the years have taught me what the days never could.

My intention was to leave my addiction in America and the timing seemed practical. Before I knew it, 2 weeks went by and I found myself smoking pot with the iguanas. Literally, I would sneak into the jungle to hide from the policia and within a few minutes the iguana would surround me close enough to catch a contact high. Same song and dance; the pot led me back to the alcohol and well before Easter my addictive lifestyle was resurrected.

Things were up in the air before my plane even left America, but I did have a plan. The plan was to work as a tour guide for a company that led motorcycle tours through the Costa Rican jungle. They operated the business through an A-plus resort named Marea Brava (Angry Tide) which is located on a black sand beach a few kilometers south of Jaco. This beautiful resort had 2 swimming pools and nearly 3 dozen units that were rented to tourists for a pretty high price. Before liftoff, I had made arrangements with the owner to work guiding dirt bike tours, but by the time I landed, the job was gone. He said I was welcome to stay there though, for a price. I stuck around there for about a month, while I searched for a new plan.

During my stay at Marea Brava, the owner gave me permission to teach surfing to their guests and even use the swimming pools to get my students familiar with balancing while sitting on a surfboard. This would give them a head start before entering the ocean of motion. I found this new opportunity to be even more fun than my original plan of riding motorcycles through a hot humid jungle. My life up to that point had so many miles of Moto-X already, I could almost feel the dirt flow through my veins. I felt that I had enough dirt biking for a while, anyways.

I was in C.R., a place known for some of the best waves in the world and I knew I had plenty of surfing still in my blood. Without intending to, within weeks I went from teaching snowboarding at Mtn. High to teaching surfing in Costa Rica. These two things would not have happened if my house was not lost to a flood, I found.

The waves outside my front door on Playa Hermosa are known for their power and world famous for their consistency. The power led to lots of crazy stories where my students were at risk and not all of them escaped injury free. I was able to stay afloat on the money (colones) my surf classes brought in and on the side I was cutting hair on the beach. With these two sources of income, I felt like I could cut it here and make Costa Rica my forever, playing with nature. And turning play into pay; it just might work out.

Everything was going perfect, like a dream that you don't want to awake from, until I was bit by a mosquito and found myself wide awake in a nightmare. Dengue fever had set in and flowed through my veins. The heat became too hot and the gravity became too heavy as I was walking down a dirt road with two of my surfing students. My legs wouldn't hold and I hit the ground. At the same time I hit the dirt, the owner of Marea Brava was turning the corner on his dirt bike heading back to the resort. With lots of help I was able to get on the back of his bike. From the resort, he called for an ambulance.

I got in the ambulance, but before they drove off I got out. I managed to express my fear of 3rd world hospitalization. I was overcome with emotion and told several people that I loved them, believing that these might be my last words. I did not know for sure at the time if I had made the right decision, but I am alive to write this, so I must have.

The next several days were spent in my living quarters soaking the sheets with my sweat. The fever produced audio hallucinations. I felt like I was watching a movie through my ears. My organs started to shut down. I would struggle for 20 minutes to urinate. Some of my symptoms were similar to my brown recluse spider bite a few years prior, minus the eroding skin that the spider inflicted.

Eventually I got better and the ocean had never felt better than the day I was strong enough to swim in it again. An unforgettable freshness and relief that made all the pain and suffering worth it.

The first 40 nights in Costa Rica, I lived in a very large straw-covered shack that consisted of 9 bunkbeds in one large space and attached to that were several communal cold water showers, which somehow sometimes sloths would sneak into. This shack or maybe I should call it a villa, was well made and a very secure shelter from wind and rain, with air conditioning as well. The only thing separating the villa from the swimming pool was a bar/

kitchen and that is where I plugged in my electric guitar.

Everyday beautiful Costa Rican women (ticas) would be swimming and sunbathing in their G-string bikinis. I found the women in this country to be very friendly with hugs and kisses on every introduction. I wanted to take them for a ride, so I bought a motor scooter and often had a tica on the back. That motor scooter carried us to paradise-like waterfalls gleaming with rainbows. Sometimes those two wheels carried 4 passengers as women that friendly usually have a couple of kids in tow and I enjoyed seeing their huge smiles as they hung on the handle bars.

Costa Ricans are very trusting people and live with little or no fear. They are the furthest thing from being shy, as whistles and hoots filled my ears from time to time. Not having to make the 1st move was quite a relief. My luck with the ladies in America was not even comparable. I liked it at Marea Brava, but I wanted a place of my own. Those 18 beds would constantly have different sleepers in them and sometimes sleep was hard to come by. It was time for my scooter and me to find a new location. I loved the neighborhood that is Playa Hermosa and quickly found a place on the other side of town, "Cabinas Surfside".

My cabina was a stone's throw to the ocean. Sleep was wonderful there with the sounds of the sea and when the waves were big, I could feel the ground pulsate as I drifted into slumber. Sometimes the sound of rain tap-dancing on the tin roof would be replaced by the noise the iguanas would make, though I could never tell if they were dancing or fighting as the roof rattled.

Right outside hanging from a single rope was a one-seater hammock. My motor scooter was parked 15' away. I had created a Tarzan-style trick for leaving home where I would swing with just the strength of my arms out the front door across the patio and land on the seat of my scooter. Super slick trick, especially this one day after a rain when the wet seat made me slip, slamming my ass to the ground. I just happened to have an audience that day and these girls got quite a good laugh.

Seemed I was always pulling off some sort of physical comedy that entire year. Body language was a great substitute until I could get a grip on the Spanish language. The view from my home was black sand beach with blue water waves and little itsy bitsy teenie weenie yellow polka dot bikinis all day long. The nights were filled with live music coming from the "Back Yard Bar and Grill" three doors down.

I made friends with one of the bands that played at this bar. Thomas (Tow-mas) was a big bald good timing gringo and the leader of the band. We would bump into each other in different towns across the country as we were both wandering about while watching the seasons change.

One night at the "Back Yard", Thomas was tripping on magic mushrooms, but was still playing an amazing guitar. His drummer was some character from Germany, named Wolfgang and on bass was a friendly Tico. Together the 4 of us played a song I wrote with my band, I K.W.I.T. Magic mushrooms and magic moments went down that night. My singing isn't that great usually. That night everything fell into its cosmic place and time. The compliments I received from the ladies went to my head and I felt like a rock star! Women just saw me differently here than they did in the States.

My new home put me in a rock 'n roll state of mind. The tin-topped roof was supported by yellowish brown cobble stone walls coming up from an emerald green marble tile floor. The textures of this structure enhanced the warm sounds of my echo-ish electric guitar. Living the rock star lifestyle located between world class waves and a deep dark jungle. Lurking in the thick floral, lived monkeys and black panthers and I often wondered if they could hear my guitar screaming sounds through their sharp acute ears. Just down the road lived a local crocodile in a small sanctuary. I would ride my scooter up to it, close enough to feel a thrill, always keeping the key ready to turn, just in case his tune turned.

"Pura Vida" means pure life. The phrase is often used by the ticos to express "live pure". A slogan similar to Hawaii's "Aloha" or the Philippines "Mabuhay". You can taste this in their food; it has a unique pureness. The cows and chickens tasted different and it took me some time to acquire an appetite for them. My American palette was much more accustomed to saturated fats, which were non-existent in the parts of Costa Rica where I found myself.

As life consumes life to sustain life, I noticed that when things don't get better they usually get worse normally during the best of times. This would be the case every time I quit quitting alcohol. Partying like a rock star takes practice, which comes naturally to a practicing alcoholic.

Found in Latin America is "guaro", a clear liquid liquor made from distilled sugar cane. The locals call it "agua loco" meaning "crazy water". And after drinking it, I would not feel sane or any pain. It was now my D.O.C. (drug of choice). Mixing it 50/50 with Gatorade would produce a 51/50 reaction in my behavior. The next day this crazy water would provide me with hours of nausea and weakness.

Surfing was often my cure for the guaranteed hangovers. The adrenaline would override the pain, but I would need to catch that 1st wave first. Vomiting in the water while afloat was also very common, not to be mistaken for sea sickness. I often wondered if my regurgitated food would attract sharks. I did notice that this revulsion would cause the other surfers to paddle away, leaving my wave selections a lot less crowded. Always I have found the bright side to every situation.

This one morning my hang-over (with-draw) was distressingly bad with a serious migraine. I really wanted to shake it off in the ocean, but that day the waves were huge and the conditions terrible for surfing, closing out and the riptide was fierce. Nobody was in the water and it was then that I made a terrible decision.

The plan was to swim out just a little bit, to feel O.K. again, but the riptide sucked me out to sea too quickly. I swam harder than I ever had before toward the shore, but I was getting nowhere and literally losing ground. Sometimes people go missing in Costa Rica and often foul play is to blame and other times the ocean is guilty of taking these lives. The ocean's pure strength is imminent and non-selective. I put myself in its wrath with no one and nothing to blame, except maybe alcohol.

Here came that familiar feeling again, that this might be the day that I die.

I was exhausted to the point that passing out was possible and at this point I was only 15 feet from land. The strong riptide current was relentless. That pulled me to remember my Lenten resolution, not to drink alcohol. Had I kept that promise made to God and myself, I would have had the strength to swim in. Had I stayed sober, this scenario would not have even come into existence.

Finally making it close enough to shore, I planted my feet. It was then that I believed continuing life on land was possible. Those last few steps to shore simulated the slipping away from the grip of a salty grim reaper. I stumbled up the beach to the dry sand and collapsed face up. Looking at the sky towards the heavens, I contemplated getting sober, again. But by that afternoon I was drunk, again.

I have seen alcoholism kill many people in many different ways. Usually in indirect ways. A phantom spirit, if you will. Alcohol is often referred to as spirits. Many times I've felt like I was dodging its metaphoric bullet, as I got loaded with every shot.

Like it or not, immigration laws would disrupt my life in C.R. every 3 months, by requiring me to vacate their country for 3 days. The invisible hands that push these rules are blind to the fact that this is freedom robbery. Some believe segregation is the answer. Some believe it is the problem. Perhaps someday we will know the truth. When freedom is only for the selected, it is easy to see it as a privilege granted to those lucky enough to be born on the right side of an imaginary line and a punishment to the others. Once again, these stories are believed by the masses, making them our intersubjective reality.

For my 1st forced trip I would head north to Nicaragua. I decided to take a bus, for this would be a journey of too much distance for my scooter. As I was getting directions to the bus station from a neighbor, he told me this story.

An elderly lady carrying a live chicken was trying to enter this bus going to Nicaragua. The bus driver stopped her and told her to read the sign "No livestock aboard". She looked at him for a moment and then without even a reply, she swung the chicken and smacked it dead upon the front bumper of the bus. Then she climbed aboard with the now dead poultry, with nothing ever really needing to be discussed.

My three days in Nicaragua were fairly uneventful. But, on that bus looking out the window, two things really stood out. First to fill my eyes was the poverty and destitution of the people living without the basic necessities. Second, was the oppressive heat, you could visually see the sun melting car tires that were placed on these people's tin-roofed homes. I imagine it is the weight of the melted rubber that keeps their roofs from blowing off.

Three months later to fulfill immigration demands, I headed south-bound for Panama. Arriving at the border after midnight added suspense to the unknown dangers that I may encounter. I passed the processing requirements and quickly found a motel.

I noticed a strong police presence here. Panama accepts the American dollar and the minimum wage for hard labor is only one dollar an hour. This is very upsetting to the workers who are born here. Walking through town on my 2nd day, I noticed a mob of angry protestors all wearing red t-shirts. As I was trying to get closer to the scene, three military officers stopped me as they noticed I was looking out of place there. With looks of concern in their eyes, they ordered me to go back to my motel room because things were going to get very serious in a few moments. As soon as I entered my room I quickly turned on the T.V. and saw a labor strike in full force. The news was rolling live footage focused on the same corner I had just walked away from.

Then, boom, boom, boom, I heard gun shots through the T.V. as well as the actual sounds of gun shots vibrating through the motel windows. The T.V. screen showed a few of the red shirt wearing protestors hitting the ground. I was overcome by the deep emotional impact this had on me, being so close to the action. I actually teared up knowing that several of the people I saw alive on the street moments earlier were now dead. And, they were murdered just because they wanted to earn more than a buck an hour.

I wanted out of that country as soon as possible and the next day my obligations to the immigration authorities were fulfilled. But finding a bus ride back to Costa Rica turned into another nightmare. The only bus was to pass by a location a half mile from my motel at 3 a.m. Too close to hire a taxi, but pretty far to drag luggage in the middle of the night. Nevertheless I walked to the bus stop sign alone on a dark empty corner. Getting there early, strangely I noticed that I was the only one waiting. The bus driver was on time. We had eye contact, but he didn't stop as I heard him accelerate leaving me with my mouth wide open and my eyes half shut.

Frustrated, confused and uncomfortable, I went back to the motel. I tried the next night, but it was the same guy and he did the same thing. Now I was going on 5 days in a place I didn't want to be. Finally losing all hope that that bus driver was not the devil himself, I got a taxi to the airport and flew back to C.R. to the comforts of home sweet home (Casa Dulce Casa).

Loco Lucas, was one of a kind. He owned and operated a surf shop a stone's throw from my cabina. Lucas is a surfer from Lake Michigan, the first and last one I have ever met. Lake Michigan is enormous enough to produce fresh water waves. When Lucas lives in the U.S., he hunts large game, skinning the animals himself, eats the meat and sells the fur. Ironic, because I remember him telling me, "Once you enter the ocean, you have thrown yourself into the food chain".

One day Lucas and I were surfing in front of our places on Playa Hermosa as the rain was pouring down pretty thick. Normally surfing in the rain is no big deal. I mean you're wet anyway. But, there was lightning and thunder as well on this occasion, yet windless, and the waves were of a very large size. The heavier the waves, the harder you work. The harder you work, the heavier you breathe. My breathing became so heavy and the rain so thick that I was ingesting enough water to cause some anxiety. I looked at Lucas and said, "It feels like I'm drowning and I'm still above sea level. I think I need to get out!" He laughed and said that I would be fine. Part of me didn't want to get out as the waves were perfect. I contemplated staying in the water, not wanting to leave my friend out in this situation alone. But, reluctantly under a dark and wet sky, I headed toward shore. As I paddled in I was thinking Loco Lucas really lives up to his name. And, now out there on his own, his chances of becoming part of the food chain had just doubled.

During the summer solstice on the day of the equinox, there was a "Soul Surfer" surf contest at Playa Hermosa, sponsored by the Back Yard Bar 'n Grill and several local surf shops. Prizes were given away after the competition for different categories such as best style, best wipeout, best tube ride and so on. As I pulled my competition jersey over my head, I could see that the waves were well overhead, powerful, thick and hollow that day. Honestly, I was more than concerned that fear might take the fun out of this day. But, like many other days, I knew that if I paddled past the fear, paradise awaited. And, also like many other days, I had a severe hangover. I was vomiting behind the palm trees right before my heat. I wasn't sure if it was because of my anxiety or my alcoholism, probably a lot of both.

This was a big event and I could hear my name being announced through the loud speaker as I sat in the water. The announcer "Skinny" was barely holding it together. He was a friend of mine as well and had told me that about an hour prior to the contest he had eaten some magic mushrooms. The beach was packed; this was by far the most spectators that had ever watched me surf. And almost as if on cue, this huge wave was heading my way and appeared to have my name on it. So, I paddled hard and dropped into a very steep vertical wall of water darkened by shadow as it eclipsed the summer solstice.

This was an opportunity to cash in on a prize. This wave was forming up to be the best tube, best wipeout or best something. The perfect position lined up as I dropped in straight legged and as erect as possible locking both hands together behind my back (stylish soul surfer stance) and entered a stand up barrel!

I heard afterwards that I almost won the prize for best style category, but I didn't. That prize went to the world renowned surfer, Jim Hogan. What I did end up with was the prize (gift bag) for the best wipeout. Every part of my body felt that wave slam me down hard. As I saw the wave closing out straight ahead of me, I pushed myself and board through the backdoor (backside of the wave). Success for a second, then the lip (top of the wave) sucked me over the falls. This forced me to hold my breath past the point of comfort, the part of surfing I enjoy the least.

Besides living through another dangerous day, I also felt a sense of accomplishment. I had received the recognition that comes with surfing amongst stand up men in the sport, even if crashing was what got me noticed. After all, this was very similar to what got me noticed in the world of Moto-X. This may sound like something a volunteer stunt man would say and I have always said, "If you don't ever fall, you will never know your limits". And by getting back up and trying again, you can exceed your limitations.

Some say it has something to do with the climate, but Perez Zeldon was rumored to have an unbalanced population of 8 women to every 1 man. And 7 out of 8 of these women were completely gorgeous. It felt like I was on the scene of a very attractive episode of the "twilight zone".

The journey from Playa Hermosa to Perez Zeldon was too far (4-1/2 hours) to bring my surfboard, guitar and skateboard on my scooter. And, I wanted all of these things with me when I arrived in Perez Zeldon. So, I hired a van and driver to haul everything including my motor scooter to my new temporary neighborhood. Having the scooter there was essential due to the fact that the closest surf was over an hour away from this town in the mountains.

It's a steep and winding road to Playa Dominical. On a weekly basis, I would travel this road on my scooter carrying a surfboard to spend a few days getting my surf fix. I had been surfing on a daily basis for months now, and if I went more than a few days without paddling, my arms would often have visible muscle spasms. This was a physical sign that my body was having withdrawal symptoms from the missed doses of salt water.

Mi espanol was advancing y mi nuevo amigo, Luis, was a big help. I remember him saying, "Vicente, when you are drunk your English is about as understandable as your Spanish is sober". Luis would help me read a few love letters that were slid under my door and assist me with writing romantic responses.

Riding my skateboard through the town's center, I heard someone yell out, "Hey, X-Gamer". That was Luis, and that's how we met and he became a great friend for the duration of my life in Perez Zeldon. Luis did not drink alcohol. He said it caused him to gamble and that lead to insanity for him. He did smoke pot though and he sold tons of it.

One day he needed a ride to pick up a backpack full of marijuana, so we got on my scooter together and the deal went down smoothly. On a side note, this was the 1st and last time I've seen cockfighters shoot cocaine down a rooster's throat. Something I didn't expect to see in the middle of a drug deal. The scene there was trippy. As we were leaving, I was thinking that this cock is going to win the fight or have a heart attack. Either way a bird is going to die.

On our way back through town, we were sitting in traffic as we were drug trafficking. This is when Luis spotted a man, a dangerous man that had been looking for him because of an unpaid gambling debt Luis had made a few months prior when he was drunk. Luis jumped off the back of my scooter and as he took his backpack off, he tells me to take the large amount of illegal drugs back to his house. I really had no choice; it all happened faster than I could process. So, I swung the pack onto my back and headed toward his house hoping that it would only be a bird that dies today. Meanwhile Luis was being chased through the streets of Perez Zeldon. And, once again, I found it hard to know which is more dangerous, the land or the sea?

After an hour long scooter ride down the winding canyon road, I arrived to a slightly wet Dominical, and checked into a motel and then went to check out the surf. The waves were breaking really far from shore and I couldn't get a clear appraisal of their size. There appeared to be nobody in the water, but I thought if I paddled way out there, there might be. As I paddled for at least 30 minutes to get out there, I was starting to realize that it was bigger than I had guesstimated.

The rain stayed consistently light, but by no means was it cold. I was in the tropics right on the equator and often the ocean water seemed too warm. I started sweating bullets of anxiety once I admitted to myself that I was scared by the size and power of this empty ocean. I had a decision to make, catch a wave in or start paddling to shore. By paddling to shore I was at risk of getting gobbled up by huge turbulent walls of white water that had the power to rip my board from my hands and force me to hold my breath for who knows how long.

Finally, I decided to catch one of these beasts, which were growing in size the longer I waited. I spotted my ride home, back to solid earth. As I was paddling into the steep and fierce wall of water, I looked to my right across the shoulder of the wave and made eye contact with another lone surfer. This would be our first and last wide-eyed sight of each other. We both held that savage expression of survival. The size and power of these waves had grown to be beyond fun. They passed that point of relaxing leisure, to a point of certain seriousness.

Drop-in time was upon me and I did so, perfectly, with a huge scream- ing lip of a barrel chasing me down as I shot out like a bullet right across this picturesque bowel. The actual speed felt comparable to the momentum I experienced when in 3th or 4th gear on a dirt bike. I traveled for quite some distance without the thought of trying to pull off any tricks. The trick here was to get out of the ocean alive today.

The wave was approaching a connecting peak that was coming in with the same swell, so it was starting to wall up into a close-out. Once again, I had two choices. First option was to point the board toward shore and race the white water before it inevitably would eat me up. I took the second option and exited the wave by aiming back out to sea. At this point I was twice as close to the shore as I was a minute before. By now the adrenaline had consumed the fear and the dry sand was as near as my next beer.

At the bar on the beach, still high from the potentially dangerous surf, I met Celin. Most of my relationships with Costa Rican women were "heat of the moment" situations. Though a few of them did become a girlfriend status, serous enough to require a break-up before moving on. With Celin, it was a spontaneous heat of the moment attraction and a somewhat lasting one as we did stuff that couples do, such as go out on dates and we even went to church on one occasion. The whole time we were together I never understood what she was saying. My Spanish was good enough to get my point across, but my comprehension level was low.

So, still high on adrenaline from the big lonely surf session and still wet, I met Celin. She lived in Perez Zeldon but was visiting Playa Dominical with her boss and another girl. Celin was only 24 at the time and 17 years my junior. These 3 girls had spent the previous night sleeping in their boss's car. All 3 of them had jobs, but still not enough money to afford a motel.

It is a shame to know that hard working people still have to live in poverty, but this is the norm in developing countries. Celin is a wonderful seamstress and even tailored her own clothes. I can still picture the home-made light blue mini-falda (mini-skirt) that she was wearing as we went out dancing that night. Dancing is huge in C.R. They take it as serious as a sport, a very seductive sport. After I bought the four of us dinner, we went back to my motel and I got another room for her friends while Celin and I spent the first of many nights together.

I like to believe that I have been with some very beautiful women in my lifetime, but Celin was next level gorgeous. No way would the two of us have been sized up together in the States. A popular American belief is that the women overseas only want a free ride and a way out of the 3rd world. I found this to be untrue. Of course, no one prefers to live in poverty while working a full time job. And, to bring her or any of many back to the U.S.A. did sound like a pretty good idea.

More than once I have experienced the pain of leaving a culture and country. Everything familiar disappears, especially your family. And from what I've seen in these impoverished countries, family is more important than money. To leave everyone and everything you know is a little like dying, while still being able to make phone calls from heaven.

Sure, life is difficult here, there and everywhere in between. Costa Rica is a paradise in so many ways and most of the girls I met there would prefer to stay than leave for the all elusive U.S.A. To the many people that feel the world begins in New York City and ends in L.A., good for you. But, what I have learned by spending so many years out of the U.S. is that the grass is greener wherever you water the soil.

In most underdeveloped countries, there are more people than beds. I have seen places in the Philippines where a family has to take shifts to sleep, a problem brought on by the combination of overpopulation and poverty. Only so many people can fit in one bed. This is not even a thought that would cross most American minds.

Heat of the moment attraction will only take a relationship so far. Mine and Celin's had gone its distance, short, but oh so sweet. Celin was one of the working class in Costa Rica who was bedless. So, as kind of a parting gift, I bought her a bed of her own. Her not wanting to "disrupt our lives" as her letter read in Spanish said, the two of our paths went in different directions. And, with no regrets, I am sure glad our trails crossed.

My Godmother, Linda 1966

Stop, Mom; We got this! 1968

Mexico 1982 Uncle Greg reattaching surfboards litte brother Scott
in the passenger seat

First skate pic on first
makeshift ramp

First Surfing Photo
1982 Mexico

Maligaya sa Manila - Happy Living Life

"Pura Vida" - Costa Rica 2007

Philippines Province Adventures

All Washed Up

Launching off skateboard ramp for
Dirt Bike Magazine

Hitting a metal freestyle jump ramp

Golden State
Motocross
Championship 2002

Footplants

Castaic "Race Around the Lake"
early 90's

Ojai Skate Park in my mid 50's

World famous
"keyhole" pool
Del Mar Skate Park
mid 80's

Shadows, dancing ghosts
from the sun

Philippines Pump Track/Bike
Park in my early 50's

First halfpipe at my parents house
early 80's on a custom painted
board by Drat

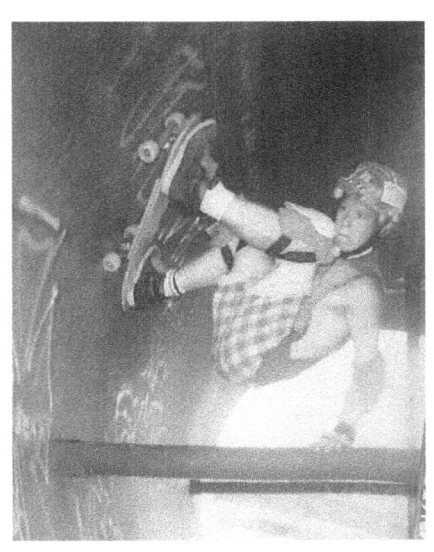

"Vertical", living up to
my nickname

Hitching a ride in Manila

Boneless Footplant during a triple
run with Mike McGill and
Don Szabo

Inverted - late 80's

LA Times
2 years in a row 1986 - 1987

Mountain High photo by Scott Starr

Bending some necks - early 90's

Matt Donovan launching into
Tahoe airspace

Tahoe Contest Manuver on
"Prop" snowboard

Costa Rica 2006 -2007

"Always looking forward to looking back"

"Tie a knot and hang on"

Hawaii October 2006
Earthquake/Landslide

Doing some volunteer stunt work

"The whole world in my hands",
Costa Rica, 2007

My Mahal, My Miracle

AA chips
Like Father, Like Son
"The apple doesn't fall far from the tree"

Mondays with Mom

Following my beautiful wife
to the other side of the world

The beautiful, strong women in my
life, Yolly, Aunt Linda, Aunt Pat,
my mom Judy, at Silver Strand

Me, Scott, Darrin - enjoying another
poolman meeting

Don Szabo and me enjoying his
second tour to the Philippines

My first introduction
to public writing

CHAPTER 9

COSTA RICA (EXTENDED) PURA VIDA!

" . . . . . . .and tomorrow the same "

Paul Minton is the type of surfer that you read about in books, and as you continue, you will. Like so many surfers, Paul owned a van. But, not like so many surfers, Paul drove his from his home state of Florida to Texas, then headed south through Mexico, Guatemala, El Salvador, Honduras and Nicaragua to Costa Rica. Paul made his migration in that van packed solid with surfboards that he shaped and glassed himself (Minton Surfboards) and by the time I met him he was an established resident of Costa Rica. As an expat, Paul continues to shape surfboards and makes a living selling and renting his surfboards as well as supplying surf lessons to the tourists.

We shared so many adventures together. Where to begin? I guess I can turn the key to get things started by rolling down the road in his van. I can't recall where we were coming from or where we were going, but I do remember how dark it was that night as we were on the highway far from anything. No street lights, only our headlights illuminating the horizon. And as we headed up an incline, it appeared to be trees that we were heading toward. It looked like thin tree trunks as the headlights passed through, then two feet above it was thick darkness. But soon we would see that things were not as they appeared to be. And as we got closer, these tree trunks started moving.

The angle we had was illusive and as we were making our way up this incline, we began to realize that this illusory vision we saw was actually cattle trotting with momentum down the highway heading straight towards the van in the black of night. Paul got on the brakes hard enough to make me clutch the 2-1/2 gallon gas can I had between my legs in hopes that it wouldn't fall over, being I had lost the gas cap and it was now only sealed with a piece of plastic and a rubber band; this was important. It was a close call, but no spill yet.

Cows and even bulls were passing by us on the left and right. Our headlights were freaking them out and causing them confusion. This one poor confused cow ran full speed right in between our headlights, dead-center into the grill, just under the front windshield. The impact was great enough to send my can of gasoline crashing to the floorboard, splashing all over Paul's van. Bewildered, the cow backed up, shook its head and tried to pass through the headlights once again. Quickly to reduce their confusion, Paul turned off the headlights. But it was too late for this cow having had his lights knocked out already. The odor of gasoline stayed in the van for a while. This actually improved the scent that pre-existed in this old van. The tropical climate always has a way to amplify an already pungent smell.

I first met Paul in Esterillos Oeste, under the roof of a pizza/bar open-air restaurant where he was renting out his personal belongings to tourists that needed beach supplies. As he looked up from reading a book, I said "Ola" and rented a longboard from him. In front of the pizza place the waves were peeling off of a point break and on the tip of this point break stands a 20 foot statue of a mermaid (La Serena). At high tide the waves splash up to her ass and at low tide you can walk out to it and climb up onto her slippery surface.

After my fill of waves, I returned his board, feeling stoked. After many words with Paul, I felt that we were going to be friends. Soon after that day I moved to Esterillos Oeste. I had enough of Playa Hermosa's pounding and often frightening beach break and Paul's neighborhood had great waves that were a little less threatening most of the time. Esterillos Oeste is truly a Costa Rican small town in the sense that it is very secluded with a very low population. The community was very friendly and it seemed like everyone knew everyone. And if I saw a new face, usually they were just passing through the place.

The owner of the pizza place let Paul and I build a skateboard half pipe ramp under this open-aired/roofed restaurant located 100 yards away from the edge of the salty surf. Such an epic time and space in my life, better than any picture that I could have redrawn for my future. Picture a snake wrapped around a teenager's neck as he drops into skate the ramp and you would see the restaurant owner's son. A snake he found in the jungle and turned into a pet. His dad used to cook chicharrones in a huge vat and as he stirred the pork fat just several feet from the ramp, I could see the dust flying from my frontside grinds adding some skate style seasoning to the special of the day.

Paul and I hung out every day for most of the year. He had become a friend of a lifetime, one of the best I have ever had. We spent so much time surfing together that we understood each other's style. This understanding made it very comfortable to share big waves together and because of our opposite stances, (Paul's right foot forward, goofy) and (my left foot forward, regular), we could see the line the other was taking. Drawing figure eights with our wakes, crossing right in front of each other with complete confidence in the other's competence.

The camera's eye catches things that the human eye misses. And the stories about saltwater crocodiles in Costa Rica are much more than myths. If you spend enough time in C.R., you are sure to meet some people with extensive scarring and those are the lucky ones. A guy on the beach showed me a picture that he had taken of his son surfing at Playa Hermosa. He discovered upon development that a pair of crocodile eyes were lurking in the face of this wave. People who have flown in helicopters above this stretch of ocean have reported seeing a great number of sharks and crocodiles. This goes to show how rewarding the rush of surfing is, that the risk is worth the reward, no matter what the price for the prize may be.

Paul from time to time would drive us to different locations where we would charter small boats that could take us to surf breaks that were inaccessible by land. For a few colones, the boat driver would take us to the surf spots, drop us off, then he would drop a line and be fishing an eye's view away while we surfed. Timing the tide was very crucial at some spots, as a shallow reef would appear when the tide was too low.

Timing is everything. And, I had good and bad timing on this day at Escondido (hidden) surf spot. As the driver got close to the waves, I could see a swell rising behind our boat. If I jumped out of the boat with my board under my belly and paddled hard, I would be riding that swell when it peaked into a wave. Gathered in a pack with a pecking order, there was a group of surfers waiting patiently for this swell to develop. As they looked at me, I realized that my impeccable timing might have appeared arrogant, but I was just in the right place at the right time. And with one fluid motion, I jumped from boat to wave with intent, leaving some jaws dropped at the audacity that had occurred. No one said anything and I myself even felt speechless. A wave I will always reminisce, even as I ride into the seas of senility.

Then came the bad timing (possibly karma). Paul and I realized that we had less than an hour of surfing left before the tide would be too low. Escondido broke mostly to the left. Going right was possible, but more dangerous because of the shallowness of the water in that direction. I couldn't resist when Paul went left off the peak. I went right. I was gliding at an accelerated pace and holding a very stable stance when "BOOM", I hit something, something that had slowed my speed down considerably. I was surprised that I did not fall.

First thing that came to mind was that I had hit a shark or crocodile. Whatever it was, it was over and done with, so I caught another wave. On this next wave my board turned very strangely, performing with an unbalanced feeling. I flipped my board over to investigate and discovered that I was missing one of my 3 fins. The right fin near the toe rail was gone. Thinking back to the wave before when I assumed that I had hit some large sea life, I had to conclude that what I actually hit was the ocean floor's live coral. So, I paddled out to where our boat driver was fishing and removed the heel rail side fin and rode the board as a single fin for the last few waves before the tide dropped below any reasonable rideable depth.

In many ways, Costa Rica is not far from animation. On land the greenery appears fluorescent at times. And, there is so much sea life in those waters, something is always moving and you just kind of get used to it. Groups of flying stingray would often jump out into the sky right in front of us always from the exact spot that the previous stingray did, like a conga line. It looked so trippy because you would only see one at a time in the exact same spot. This made it seem like there was only one stingray just doing 360 ⌧ revolutions over and over again. Another vivid wildlife memory I hold is seeing Paul put his two hands together to gather up a very small seahorse. Aquaman came to mind.

In between waves back on land while exploring through the jungle not knowing exactly where we were going, we found this spectacular waterfall. Tres Piscinas (Three Pools) appeared after quite a hike and once you saw it you could see how the name came into play. This waterfall had 3 stages to it, each level collecting enough water to fill a swimming pool. The top pool had a huge tree next to it. This tree lurched and hovered about 25 feet above the deep water. Paul with his Tarzan-type persona was the first to go, launching himself airborne off the trees limb and into the brisk clear water. After the very hot and humid hike into this tropical oasis, the colder-than-ocean fresh water was truly refreshing.

There was another surf spot on our "surf it" (bucket) list called "The Island". This place would only break when the swells got really big. And the time came when the conditions all lined up. Paddling out to this line up was possible, but most chose to hire a small boat. "The Island' is just that, a small island not too far from the mainland of C.R. So close in fact that many opted to paddle back and that is what we did. Wait a minute! I'm getting ahead of myself; back to the boat.

On this boat we shared the ride with a few other expats from what other countries I cannot remember. I do recall that they appeared hardcore and well prepared for the large-sized surf that we were all headed for. I, on the other hand, was a bit nervous, actually a lot nervous up to my throat with anxiety. I knew I had skills, but I am far from the type of surfer that could drop into Hawaii's "Pipe Line" or California's "Mavericks". The size on this day was pushing my limits; needle to the red. Adrenaline overrode my fear and I felt much better after catching a few waves as the nausea went away.

At "The Island" all the waves broke to the left (backside for me). Going right was not an option. The waves literally broke off the face of the cliff that the island provided. The volumes of water attached to the pounding sounds of erosion triggered a flashback thought, that water had washed my house away and somehow I drifted to here for now. This whole day my eyes were wide open, even while duck-diving under these two story high walls of water.

And, what I saw next led me to believe that Paul's day was going to end early. A wipeout caused the string that holds his leash to the board to break. This very rare circumstance left him separated from his board. Floating about 50 feet apart from each other, Paul had to reconnect with his board before the next wave could grab it and possibly sweep it to the distant shore. Swimming as fast as humanly possible, he achieved this vital task. It would be normally unusual to have an extra 4 inches piece of string with you to re-attach a leash to a board, unless you considered using the string that keeps your surf trunks above your butt, which would lead to other problems. But like an "aha moment", Paul reached into his surf trunks back pocket and pulled out an extra 4 inch leash attachment string, like "Whallah!". As I had witnessed with Paul throughout the year, he lived a magical life of a minimalist. Getting by on very little, yet all his needs came to fruition. It was beautiful to watch.

So far, a jaw dropping, eyes wide open kind of day. After we surfed a few more really big waves, we headed back for the long paddle to shore and then a long 45 minute hike back to the van. The hike turned into well over an hour because we kept stopping to sit on the rocks and just look back at "The Island" to reflect on what had just happened. Not to mention the two topless girls we saw swimming, resembling mermaids. The hours of peace were received after the moments of anxiety had passed, achieved and well-deserved. The contrast between the two emotions are so extreme that I can only describe it as passing from a nightmare into a dream as you flip the pillow over.

Psilocybin is the active ingredient in magic mushrooms. And after experimentations with L.S.D. (acid), I must conclude that the experiences are very similar between these two hallucinogens. Shrooms and acid provide a great trip for some people, some of the time, but not all of the people every time. Bad trips do exist with both of these drugs. With magic mushrooms, the amount of psilocybin varies from one mushroom to the next. To the naked eye, it is really a gamble on how much of the active ingredient you will be digesting.

Stemming straight from cow crap, these types of mushrooms grow abundantly in Costa Rica. The taste is horrible, but doable. Some friends had picked an abundance of these shrooms and needed freezer space to keep them fresh. So I moved the ice tray to the side and stocked my fridge full of them. Then I picked a day to go on a solo adventure to a waterfall and enjoy the state of mind that often comes with magic mushrooms. Enjoyable at first, yes, then things took a twist.

I took off down the highway on my scooter after eating a few shrooms, but the feeling was not coming on very strong. My alcoholic thinking told me that more would be better, so I turned around, ate a few more and got back on my scooter. Well, the extra few I ate must have been more potent than my first indulgence because I experienced a lift off that I was not prepared for. I was flying so high that I couldn't even feel my tires touching the pavement. And, as I was floating down the highway I started noticing how fluorescent green the already green jungle was. Then, I started to think, "Oh no! What if I ate too many shrooms?" Earlier that day someone had mentioned that their friend was never the same after his shroom trip. Maybe the power of suggestion triggered my paranoia. Whatever it was, it was reasonable to consider that that had turned my good trip into a bad trip. This consideration made it reasonable to abort my waterfall mission.

I felt my scooter's momentum flowing forward, as it was, but it appeared as though I was going backwards, similar to a kaleidoscope. That's when I decided to stop, and I did. But the road did not as the motion seemed to last awhile. Nothing was as it seemed. I was in full hallucination mode. Somehow I made it back to my cabina where I knew I was way too high to be healthy. Negative thoughts started flooding my head and I began to think that I had gone too far this time and gave myself brain damage. Only time would tell and shrooms are known to last 5 to 10 hours.

I waited it out, not enjoying a minute of it. The cobbled stone rocks that made up the interior wall of my home started having sex with each other, but that is as pleasant as it got. That trip would be my last, and it was. Fear, as much as I hate it, has taught me some valuable lessons. I know I am sane now, but truthfully if I look at something with a pattern for too long it starts to dance around, even to this day.

There is no way to fit an entire life into one book and I have had to leave many stories out. This next short segment I was going to leave out. Fact is, I had forgotten about it until I went bicycle riding in between writing sessions here in the Philippines.

After a rain, on the slick concrete while trying a new freestyle trick, I slipped and landed hard on the back of my skull. My head started bleeding, instantly jarring my memory. The pain, the blood, the instant lump on my head all brought back memories of a solo surf session I had 12 years prior at "El Pescador's" (The Fisherman's) Beach, Costa Rica.

Just walking distance from my home in Esterillos Oeste, the fisherman would clean their catch, leaving the guts and fish heads floating in the shallow waters. One day the waves were inviting and no one was in the water or even on the beach. Quiet and eerie was the atmosphere as I remember. I was up to my knees in the ocean when I noticed the fish heads and not so clear water surrounding me, but the waves looked good and I wanted to surf. I thought about turning around, but my feet were already wet. The sight of fish death carried an omen.

I paddled through the gloomy water, which carried a heavy stench and when I got out to the waves everything seemed fine. Though in my mind something felt off, so I decided to only catch 3 waves and call it a day. On my 3rd and final wave, I found myself with a promising tube ride ahead. My board got too high on the wall (face of the wave) and together we got sucked up into the temporary vertical current that constructed this wave. This threw the board from under my feet to over my head. And, as I fell into the water, the board travelled with the lip of the tube and reconnected with my head.

The smack on the skull impact was exactly as hard as the hit I took to the cement from my bicycle 12 years later, which reminded me to tell you this story. Another similarity between both of these stories is that people who saw me shortly after the accidents all told me to go to the hospital. In both situations I'm sure stitches would have been applied, but it was my decision and I declined. When I am outside of America, I try to stay outside of the hospitals. Now I wear scars on my skull from all around the world.

I am well into my 50's and still sustain injuries while chasing the adrenaline high. Just the other day I was taking a breather in between these pages and went skateboarding, lost my balance and hit the ground so hard that it knocked the wind out of me, again. Most people have never experienced this sensation of a waterless drowning that comes from knocking the wind out of your body. I have done this more than a dozen times and every time it feels like it may be my last breath. This is not normal, but for me, not unusual.

I still have not decided on which would be less enjoyable, a crocodile or a shark attack. Meeting survivors of both is not that uncommon in C.R.; the scars give them away. Esterillos by definition means "the tidal mouth of a large river, where the tide meets the river's current". Esterillos Oestes's coastal terrain is good for creating excellent surf as sand bars develop in front of these rivers. Crocodiles thrive in this atmosphere, a romantic setting for breeding draws them here, I suppose. Crocodiles are not man hunters, but make no mistake they can become man-eaters. The salt water crocodile becomes very territorial around mating season and if you come too close to his perspective mate, he may become jealous and strike out of rage.

In Costa Rica it is not normally unusual to find saltwater crocodiles swimming between freshwater and brackish water. They often enter the sea from one river and swim up or down the coastline to the next river and sometimes right under unsuspecting surfers. After heavy rains, the rivers fill with mud that then washes into the ocean. A chocolate water is its appearance, but I coined the term "crocolate water". The lack of visibility in these conditions increases accidental encounters.

Paul took me to the "El Silencio" (The Secret) surf location, an hour hike up the rugged coast from Esterillos Oeste. He didn't keep it a secret from me and well, now you know also. As the tide was very low, Paul and a few other locals from town decided to wait for the tide to rise. For several reasons I neglected to understand. My American impatience could not wait as I headed out, saying that I would see them when they were done waiting.

On the map this location is called Punta Malo (Bad Point) and I could see why. It was untamed terrain with a long stretch of reef which took me quite some time to carefully walk over. This reef, my friends would soon be able to paddle over when the tide came up. The waves didn't look that big from the land, but when I got to them, about 20 minutes from the sand, they were impressively large. Thunderous crashing would vibrate my ears with the sound of each wave as I paddled closer. I will never forget how loud that surf was and how small my friends on the beach looked. I could barely spot them. And, I know now that I was way past their vision. Being the only soul in the water amplified the sound of every crashing wave.

I caught one and surfed it successfully, but on the second one, I fell. No big deal, my leash would retrieve my surfboard. I felt the tug of the leg rope for a second, then nothing! The Velcro leg attachment detached. This separation anxiety felt like a fault of mine. The lost possession of my surfboard left me wondering why I had not attached the leash to my leg more securely. Several waves transported my board to shore, thus leaving me alone in the depths of Punta Malo.

It might not be true, but for some reason having a board between me and the food chain always gave me a sense of security, and a crowd always multiplied my odds as well. But, now that my security blanket was gone, I was on my own. Thoughts of becoming shark or crocodile crap left me when the thoughts of drowning became overwhelming. It was going to be a long swim and I was getting very tired. I was hoping that my friends would spot my board, but that never happened. By the time I made it to shore alive the tide was high enough for my Costa Rican compadres to get their surf on. So, I gathered my board, ate a peanut butter sandwich, drank some fresh water and paddled back out with my friends, this time triple checking to see if my leash was properly attached to my leg.

During my year of living/surfing in C.R., I had looked down the barrel of several waves, but this would be the first time that I would look down the barrel of a gun that didn't belong to la policia. Paul and I, along with Skinny and Ariel, had just finished surfing and having a few beers. We were unloading our surfboards while parked on the side of the road in front of Skinny's house, when provoked trouble approached. The driver of the car approaching was a known enemy of Skinny's. Skinny spit on his front windshield. The car came to an abrupt stop and the rivals rushed at each other. The driver was wearing a button up shirt, which Skinny ripped open during a stumble in the rumble. This exposed a gun holstered in a shoulder strap. Spontaneously I yelled, "He's got a gun!"

Ariel is one of the most beautiful tica surfers in C.R. and you can see her modeling in the Costa Rican magazines published in 2007. After pointing the gun at Skinny, it was then turned to Ariel, who was still looking pretty as well as pretty scared by this point. Then the gun was pointed at Paul and after that it was my turn to look down the barrel of a gun. The potential shooter shouts, "Freeze or I will shoot all of you and I won't miss. I have military training!"

I had seen Skinny's enemy, whom is also an expat, a few times before around town and I never had any problems with him. But Skinny and this guy had a history that was now threatening our future.

This situation reminded me of the ongoing question that I often ponder, "Is it safer on land or in the sea?" Luckily, the fight ended as quickly as it had begun. And as the dust returned to the dirt, the gunman drove away without spitting any bullets down the barrel. We all stood there frozen in a state of shock, stunned with a strange sense of pleasure that is unavoidable every time your body produces so much adrenaline, so quickly.

That whole year I was having the time of my life and at the same time often close to having an untimely death. My drinking had gotten really heavy to the point that blood was secreting through my chest leaving tiny crustaceans on my skin like miniscule body barnacles. Several times the blood vessels in my eyes would burst leaving big red stains in my bloody eyes. The hangovers could only be cured by drinking more alcohol. I started to wonder, "How will

I die; from internal or external forces?" Explode or implode? Was I killing myself to live? This, of course, was the question, "Did I drink for pleasure or to escape pain?" The better syntax would be "drink to postpone pain". One way or another the end of the ride was coming soon. Sink or swim.

Paul had a surfboard I wanted, one of the boards that he had shaped in Florida and brought to Costa Rica. This board is as much the classic surfboard as Paul is the classic surfer. A classic single fin diamond tail with a glass job that proved to be thicker than my scalp. He wanted $500 U.S. dollars for this stick, which was reasonable. Knowing I couldn't take my motor scooter back to the U.S., I offered a trade. So, he allowed me to ride this classic single fin for a long time before the scooter became his. By then, the scooter I bought for $750 Dollars had over 7,000 kilometers of my travels on it. That scooter was a big part of my life, supplying many memories to me and to those who have been my passengers. On occasion it had even carried 4 full-sized adults going full speed.

As an expat in Costa Rica, my time was concluding. I would soon be saying some sad goodbyes to the many eyes of Esterillos Oeste. These people had become part of my life and I theirs. One neighbor named James threw me a huge going away party. And another neighbor named Pat put together a beautiful four song picture collection D.V.D. with her remarkable editing skills. The Montage was played in front of the large crowd that attended my going away party. A party that got wet 'n wild with midnight swimming filling the pool.

After the party, good and drunk, I took my scooter for one last romp. Ripping and sliding down the dirt roads, all gas or all brakes, riding like a fool with the alcohol limiting the ability of my agility. Still, somehow I walked, or I should say stumbled away from that night feeling invincible. The next morning I had almost convinced myself to miss my flight. I wanted to continue living in C.R., but continuing to stay alive here was becoming very challenging. I was tore up from the floor up and needed a checkup from the neck up! I needed some vitamin-sea, so I jumped in the ocean for some temporary relief. And, with a little help from my friends, my belongings were loaded into Paul's van and we were off to the airport.

Just outside of town, we saw a cute nica (Nicaraguan female) walking on the side of the desolate highway. She said that she was on her way to Alajuela, a town close to the airport. And after a few kilometers of conversing in our broken languages, she invited us for lunch at her home. Luckily we had a little time before my flight, so we had a home cooked meal with this pretty nica and her daughter. There was no husband in her pictures. She took a liking to me and gave me a romantic kiss that would be our first kiss and a goodbye kiss, all in one.

We made plans quickly for my return. Off the top of my spinning head, I claimed that I would return in 3 months and that we could become an instant familia in Costa Rica together. I had given her my parent's phone number and address and she mailed me sexy pictures of herself and even called me once, but I was not there.

Leaving Costa Rica on that note made me feel good and bad at the same time. Deep in my heart I felt that this may well be my last day in C.R., ever. I did not want to believe it, but even to this day I have not returned.

As for Paul Minton, I knew that I would miss him. He had become my best friend that year and we had shared such a similar mindset. On parting, I looked him in the eye and said, "It's possible that we may never see each other again in this lifetime, but as far as friendships go, it doesn't get any better than this". And, in his supercool laid back surfer way of talking, he spoke the words, "That is . . . . . . good enough for me". Pura Vida!

CHAPTER 10

GOING MOBILE/PLAYTIME

**"Down the Old Trail, Rises a New Tale.
Every man has a tale to tell as he travels
through the streets unknown" - VK**

Things were still up in the air on my flight back to California. After landing, I would soon be going down the same old roads that lead to a new tale to tell. The first form of transportation was a bus ride to the bicycle shop. After that purchase, I was down to 79 dollars. I peddled into a financially sobering realization, that life was a chain reaction, as my bicycle chain spun my wheels.

A year prior, on my flight to Costa Rica, I had a plan. But, after seeing my plan fall apart and realizing that things had turned out better there than my original plans, I landed in U.S. soil without a plan. This may not have been funny to God, for they say the way to make God laugh is to tell him your plans. Know plans or no plans, really only God knows. To many people my life may have looked like a bad joke. I remember watching my siblings and parents kind of just shaking their heads, but not laughing.

Though I still wasn't sober yet, I did have some sayings stuck in my head from the past 8 years of sporadic sobriety in A.A. meetings. One principle is "God's will, not mine." So, I moved forward while stumbling sideways. Still drunk every night and vomiting every morning. I've heard that an alcoholic can pass a lie detector test when he is asked if he believed that he would never drink again. But, belief and truth are not always congruent. My thirst for sobriety was real, but quenching it with alcohol proved to be counterproductive. And, however much I sincerely tried to stop drinking, I continued to fail myself for the next 3 years.

So, down the old trail I continued. My fortune was spent. But, fortunately, at this time in my life I held a very high credit score. And, within 2 weeks, I was rolling down the highways of Ventura, California in a home/vehicle, a 28 foot 1989 Chevy Bounder Motorhome. Roaming around for a couple more weeks. I was sort of (motor-homeless) living on the streets. Not even comparable to the 3rd World (homeless) I had just witnessed in Costa Rica. I had a shower, kitchen and a bed everywhere I went, but nowhere to park them without getting a ticket or paying a fee. Also, no income to continue going mobile.

God willing, I had found a job at the same time I was losing grip of my last dollar. God's plan was so cool. I ended up scoring a job at an R.V. storage yard named PlayTime. It was a top notch facility with an enormous indoor R.V. parking building. I quickly became the "Porter" and was in charge of parking over 300 motor-homes on a piece of property over 7 acres large in (Ventura) Oxnard, California. At PlayTime, we did everything from washing R.V.'s, filling propane to emptying septic tanks. The staff of about 10 people were all experts in their fields. One employee even custom painted some of them. We had full-time mechanics on hand and a very expensive scissor lift, also several hydraulic R.V. lifts. In one section of this extremely huge building was a retail store which sold every R.V. accessory imaginable.

My pay was only minimum wage, but the benefit was that I could live there with unlimited water and electricity, under the beautiful and fresh skies of Ventura/Oxnard. Since I was spending all night, every night there, I soon became the all-night security guard for the PlayTime establishment. And, there were nights when break-ins happened. To keep the story flowing, I won't go into detail here, but there were occasions when face to face conflicts with burglars were experienced.

Another benefit of living in this location was that my Spanish vocabulary was advancing with the help of a couple of PlayTime employees. I became somewhat fluent in that language, but in hindsight, I probably should have been learning the Filipino language, as now I find myself living in Southeast Asia needing to learn a third language – Tagalog. The Philippines, a place I've now resided long enough for most people to ask me "How long have you lived here?" Instead of "How long you visiting?" I now understand these questions in 3 languages. While asleep dreaming, I speak and listen in a mixture of all three dialects. That's how embedded into my subconscious they have become. "The years teach us what the days never could."

Back to how I ended up "Going Mobile". As I peddled up to the "For Sale" posted motorhome, I noticed that it had a bicycle rack on the front bumper and a motorcycle rack on the back. After paying the owner for the R.V., I put my bicycle on the front bumper rack. As I was doing this, I wondered how long it might take me before I could put a motorcycle on the back bumper rack.

Within 2 weeks, I had my first paycheck stub, which was a requirement to secure a motorcycle loan. And, as quick as the KTM 530cc motorcycle is fast, I had a brand new one sitting on the back bumper of my motorhome. A justifiable purchase, because driving my home around was costing about 8 miles to the gallon.

PlayTime R. V. Center would allow me to use my motorcycle for the daily errands I was sent on. Trips to the bank or to pick up parts for the R.V.'s were done with a pack on my back, popping wheelies from light to light. And, if the delivery or pickup was too large for my backpack, I would use the company truck.

So, within a month I went from living amongst 3rd World poverty, from seeing so many homeless, to being the caretaker of over 300 motorhomes, for what appeared to be millionaires. The contrast was shocking, to see these homes on wheels only being used a few weekends a year. And, even though my motorhome was the oldest and the cheapest one on the lot, I still had so much gratitude.

Sometimes in the middle of the night I would get a call to deliver a motorhome to the pick-up staging area. One night I had gone to bed after drinking a bottle of 100 proof vodka and was called to prepare a pick-up for a customer. Well, sometimes I would have to move 4 or 5 huge R. V's just to get to the one assigned. The poles that supported the roof of this enormous building were always an obstacle, and the space in between each R. V. was only 2 feet. I often referred to this situation as trying to pull the bottom cracker out of a box of saltines without knocking any salt off. Not every time, but that time, I got lucky and let's just call it a salt-free or fault-free night.

As I mentioned in an earlier chapter, every chapter is comparable to a song in this book/album. In this melody called life –

(I K.W.I.T.) Lyrics

**"Feeling the rock of my walk, more than just talk.
This I was provin' while groovin'.
Flowin' as I was growin'.
Miles were showin', but I kept goin'"**

Some songs feel like the sound tracks of our lives. So, this chapter is titled "Going Mobile" a song from The Who's "Who's Next" album. Now and then I flow from the ear to the pen, hoping you will feel the Zen.

I was comfortable living at this enormous indoor/outdoor parking facility that I called home for almost 4 years. PlayTime also stored many classic and exotic cars. People paid good money to keep their valuable assets out of the elements. We even had one section completely filled with boats. I was given a watch dog to help me patrol the security of these investments, and Rico, the dog became very useful. Some nights the sound of rain on my camper roof was soothing. But, the theft rate increased on rainy nights, making Rico and my jobs less effective, due to the drowned out sound.

It wasn't the small time burglaries that put PlayTime out of business. It was the insurance rates and a tremendously large overhead. I was sad to see the place succumb to a slow demise over that last year. I got laid off as the porter/errand runner/R.V. washer, so my paychecks stopped. But, they continued to allow me to live there. I was actually the last part of PlayTime to leave the property. I still had water and electricity, and a place to park my motorhome. So, I wasn't homeless (without an address), but, by this point, close to foodless. I needed to figure something out, as I was counting the canned goods from my kitchen cupboards.

At this point I was filling my belly with the donations made for painting street addresses on the curbs of suburbia. I had done this job in my teens from time to time. All that is needed are some stencils of numbers and some black and white paint. The day before I painted, I would leave a note on the front doors requesting a $5.00 donation for service rendered, and if they didn't want the service, just leave this note above the address on the curb. Somedays, only making enough to eat and not enough for alcohol. And, eventually my thirst led me to new ideas.

I found some occasional jobs cutting grass as a gardener, but that wasn't cutting it. Then, I recalled still having a current and valid cosmetologist license, which I had been renewing for over the last 2 decades. So, after several failed attempts, I finally found a hair salon that would hire me. At this particular establishment in Oxnard, California, they only spoke Spanish and most of the hairdressers there also had side jobs working the strawberry fields, immigrants from Mexico.

Every one of them cut hair way better than my abilities allowed. The manager didn't speak English, but he retaught me how to cut hair. And, after working there a few months, my Spanish advanced even further. I really enjoyed working there, mostly because it was only a couple blocks from a really good surfing spot. The bright side was that on my lunch breaks, I was able to catch some waves and eat some tacos. On the dim side, I wasn't able to even make minimum wage, even on my best days. In the hair business it usually is a commission deal. And, the truth was that my haircutting skills just weren't cutting it either.

A college student and some of her colleagues needed to film a documentary on the "down and out" people of Ventura County. First time I met her, she was shooting still photos while I was surfing at Rincon. She was telling me about some of her school assignments and I began to tell her about Rico and me living in the storage yard. She called a few weeks later asking if she and the class group could film an interview with me, in my home on wheels.

The available date they had, turned out to be on my 43rd birthday. Several of these aspiring film-makers in their early 20's showed up on July 29th equipped with some high dollar filming equipment, ready to record this documentary. They set up spot lights and queued up some microphones. I thought it would be a nice touch to begin the interview with the rap/poem which you had read earlier in this book, "20 years in 2 minutes". The alternative titled, "Then, Happened, Now", which is the basic storyline of the shares that you can hear at any A.A./N.A. meeting. Which include – what it was like "THEN", what "HAPPENED" and what it's like "NOW".

So, we are rolling "lights, camera, action". And, as I am rambling off this condensed version of my life filled with many natural disasters . . . . . . an earthquake hits! The suspension of my motorhome starts swaying back and forth. The timing was surreal and I started smiling as I watched young eyes widen and shocked mouths drop. The earthquake was fairly large, large enough to make the small crowd in my camper all head for the door at the same time.

As they panicked, I could not have felt more relaxed. I think it was because by that time in my life, I had learned that flowers need manure. And,

174

after all the shit that I have lived through, I had come to realize what is real in my eyes, is that the end is only an illusion that gives way to a new beginning. Like a birthday! - - - - - - - - - -

When PlayTime was at its peak, I was working 5 full days a week, and that provided enough money for the weekends, when I would gas up the motorhome. With my Moto-X bike on the back bumper, I would head out to the desert or Santa Clarita to ride some old trails with some old friends. We even got our old band back together for a few "I KWIT" sessions.

Those days were fun, but eventually I couldn't even afford gasoline to keep the motorhome rolling. Painting curbs and giving bad haircuts wouldn't cut it. I think my dad could see this. I never asked him for help, but I believe he had the foresight to see that if he donated a truck to me, that I would return to my old profession of pool service.

I found profit in his prophecy. And, in no time at all, I was back to making over $20.00 an hour. Finding a job with "Conejo Pools" was a blessing. And, once again, I used the business name "Water Wizards", to subcontract 50 swimming pools per week.

At my interview with Brian Black of Conejo Pools, we were sitting on the tailgate of my dad's donated 1989 Toyota 4x4 truck. I felt my 20 years of experience was enough to get me the job, if everything else checked out. You see, Brian was looking for an honest man that would keep the job for an extended period of time. I could see that he wanted someone for the long haul. So, in return, I helped him see that I was the man for the job. I remember giving him my word to commit to 5 years, but something "normally unusual" usually happens to me, about every 5 years. This, of course, was after I had just filled him in with a short version of my perpetually changing life. Anyhow, now looking back, I can see this may be how the title of this book came about.

Brian, who was still Mr. Black to me at this point, was wearing sunglasses. And, in a respectful and considerate manner, I asked him to remove them, so I could know him further than words would allow. And, after receiving confirmation of employment, I looked him in the eye and said "you even look like someone that I could be friends with". By that point he may have been thinking, "Man, this guy is 'normally unusual' ".

Brian and I became friends. Five years later I married a beautiful Filipina and moved to the Philippines. This brought an expression onto his face that was normally unusual, the opposite of deja-vu, somewhat a vu-ja de.

Speaking of déjà vu. Another friend pulling a dirt bike off of my stuck body, Brian became one of them. This situation was becoming about as normal as the wind getting knocked out of my body. Often times simultaneous. It is a unique dynamic when you become friends with your employer. Nevertheless, we share some tales that come with riding trails.

Brian was also there when my ultimate sobriety rooted. He witnessed my implosion, the overload and eventual breakdown of my alcoholic anxiety. This took place after the 1st year of the 5 years that I worked with him. I was cleaning swimming pools full time, but still living in the PlayTime parking lot and it was there on 12-31-10 that I experienced my last alcoholic intoxication. But, I kept sparking pot in that parking spot for six more weeks and on 2-15-11, I put the pipe down and that began and became my true sobriety date.

The next chapter, I will dedicate solely to sobriety, focusing on the solution. By now you have read enough about the complexity of the problem. But before that, I would like to squeeze in another trip crossing the Mexican border. I had a week long paid vacation coming from Conejo Pool Service, and my Aunt and Uncle had a vacation home in Gaviotas, Mexico, where some of my friends and I could stay. This was around the same time that the news was covering a multitude of beheadings south of the border, brought on by a Mexican drug cartel. They would cut off human heads and hang them from street signs and fences. Some of this was taking place right in front of my tia's y tio's vacation casa.

Well, my friends got scared and backed out of coming to Mexico with me. So, now I was a solo cholo on a mission to position myself into the sweet spot of some Mexican waves ---------- Los Gaviotas (of the seagulls) es muy hermosa and the waves break right off a world class point.

My Aunt Pat and Uncle Greg have always had a passion for Mexico. In 1982, they spent a whole year living on the tip of Baja, Cabo San Lucas. Uncle Greg was a surfer from the 60's era and a Vietnam veteran, who eventually became a pool man known as the "Agua Hombre". And in April of that year (1982), my dad flew our whole family down there for a week long vacation. This gave my mom the opportunity to visit with her sister. One morning while there, my uncle, my brother and I headed down the beach in a rail dune buggy. We thought that we had tied our surfboards to the roof. Upon arrival at the surf spot, we realized that we had forgot the knot. I will never forget the feeling of losing our surfboards. Of which, we u-turned and quickly recovered.

My Aunt Patti was only 13 years my senior. She was the youngest of my mother's sisters. We became pretty close near the last 5 or 6 years of her life. She even helped edit the first two chapters of this book. Cancer was her demise and it came quick, leaving her only months to live. The last time we were together was April, 2019, and at her hospital bed, I was able to read her a segment of my writing. At the time, coincidentally, I was writing about my philosophy on the afterlife. And if you have gotten this far, then you also have read that segment. She smiled and replied, "Vince, I am going to miss you." Then, in turn, I replied, "I will miss you more." And, in return, came another smile.

Her dad (my grandpa) used to tell her, "Give them the what for!" It took her years to understand what he meant. I translated it to mean "Question Authority". I'm not sure how she translated, "Give them what for." And, I'm not sure what Grampa meant. I wish I had asked them while I still had the chance.

To get back on course, with this border crossing story, I will return to the future past of April, 2010. Crossing the border with my boards and (buds) drugs, but without my buddies. I never felt alone or at least sad about the solitude, as long as I had my best friend (MaryJane/Bud) marijuana by my side. Sneaking drugs across the border, especially during this time period, was going to be scary, but a necessary fear that I would have to face. During this part of my life I could not face living any other way. I had no choice.

Luckily, there were other elements of danger other than possible beheadings and jail time, and this helped distract my mind. A fairly large storm was passing through Mexico and had already begun to flood the streets of Tijuana. Mentally preparing myself to surf large waves kept my thoughts positive, but I would have to wait a couple of days for the cities' sewage to drain and dilute into the ocean before the water would be clean enough to surf. That, or face another dangerous element called "infection".

First things first, and that was to cross the border. I brought 3 surfboards, 2 ice chests full of beer and 1 bag of buds. Wisely, to reduce the odds of getting caught bringing drugs across the border, I would only do it going into Mexico. And, on my way back to the U.S. I could cross the border drug-free. But, the addict in me felt uncomfortable being drug-free for more than a couple of hours. And, Ventura is about a 5 hour drive north of the border. So, I needed to stash some buds near the border on the U.S. side so that I could make the 5 hour trip home, comfortably. I put enough dope in an empty soda can and hid it in a parking lot under some bushes. This elaborate plan came natural. These are not normally unusual thoughts for an addict.

Writing about waves can be as challenging as riding them, themselves. They don't ride themselves and they don't write themselves. Waves, at times, can be described as being in the spin cycle of a saltwater washing machine and can really put your mind through the ringer. There isn't much left to this chapter, except to attempt describing one of the most memorable waves of this journey.

After a couple of days relaxing in my Aunt and Uncle's vacation home, all alone, watching big brown waves roll by, on the 3rd day I arose to big blue surf. The storm had passed leaving behind mental rainbows and beautiful empty large waves. Time to start drawing artistical lines on the canvas, which is the ocean. Surfboard, as my brush to paint this picturesque scene, leaving behind a unique signature on nature.

Leading up to every wave, there is so much that goes into them. For this particular wave, it was many miles and several kilometers. Until ultimately, the surf and the surfer became one. They both had traveled great distances through all kinds of weather to emerge into temporary togetherness. There is so much more to their wavelength than just the length of the wave. And, in my memory, this one has endured the distance.

The water was super cold, but I was prepared by wearing the full gear. Even wearing a thick wetsuit, gloves, a hoody and booties, my connection to this wild wave was felt beyond the depth of skin. My body was near numb, but my soul was on fire. Experience provided me with confidence, but at this point I knew that relying on muscle memory would be of equal importance.

From the tip of this Mexican point-break, a double overhead wave was scratching the horizon as I paddled to greet it with full conviction. From the top of this steepening slope, my drop-in went textbook, followed by a very long and drawn-out bottom turn. Intentionally, I stalled at the flat bottom in front of the wave, as this allowed the wave to catch up with me, like a ball to a glove. This was a technique that I often used to provide entrance into the pocket, the section of the wave with the most usable power. Instantaneously evaluating how the wave was lining up and what would become possible, I simultaneously collected my thoughts as I pushed a 2nd bottom turn. This lead to a vertical section where I proceeded to carve up the wall and send out a rainbow spray of H2O over the top of a feathering lip. The speed this produced launched me way ahead of the curl. Instinctively I knew this was the place for a cutback. This returned me back into the pocket, the power zone. The wave was still howling and bowling as I saw a potential barrel ride in my reach. But, by this time the wave had made it to the rocky jetty that is at the end of Los Gaviotas. I still had plenty of time to get into this tube ride, but could see that making it out alive was not going to be an option. So, while enjoying the tubing view for a few seconds, keeping one eye on the rocks, I kicked out the backdoor. In English this means, "Submerging my board and body through the back of the wave, allowing the wave to carry on toward the jetty without me." The ride ended abruptly.

CHAPTER 11

SOBERHOLIC

**"Until you can admit that something is broken,
It remains beyond repair""**

At this point in my life came the hugest change of all. A change in perception and re-conception, an altered reality. Sobriety. It was time to reroute, to reduce the odds of taking myself out. Anxiety was peaking at an all-time high, even when I was high! I was scared to death of dying. Here I would like to share some solutions that I have found to the problems of living and the answers that I needed to stay alive.

I meshed together the two words "sober" and "alcoholic" (which are an oxymoron/paradox) to name this chapter. This I did with hopes of explaining the intensity of which one would need to achieve sobriety. Every day we must be as diligent about being sober as we were about getting wasted. I had been trying to stop since I started, without ever achieving continued success. Many times going extended periods without drugs/alcohol. Often 3 months, several times 6 months and even a few 8 month periods. I was able to sustain temporary sobriety, but never a whole year. While attending meetings, I watched many alcoholics receive 9 month chips. And as of writing this with over 12 years sober, I have only one 9 month chip. I honestly don't think that I could do it again and this helps keep me clean and sober. In the end I realized, mathematically, that I wouldn't have enough life left to achieve 9 months again if history were to repeat itself, as it often does.

If you are truly an addict/alcoholic, then there will come a day when you will no longer be able to drink or use. It is just better to be alive when that day comes. It may sound like I am just being dramatic and exaggerating about how close to the edge that I had become. Other sources would have confirmed the same verdict. Close friends had said they were getting afraid to party with me. Some said, "You're barely alive".

Making this story hard to believe possible was the fact that I was still active in my extreme sports. Puking was usually involved, but my addiction to adrenaline was not ready to retire. Mental illness often goes undetected and addiction, I include as one. We become as sneaky as our disease. And, recovery was required for me to sneak past the creepy grim reaper.

The "Alice in Chains" album cover, "Jar of Flies" reminds me of this science project. Several flies were put into a jar with a vented lid. The flies would continue to bounce off the lid and back to the bottom as they flew to the top to escape. After allowing them to do this for several attempts, the scientist removed the lid. But, not even one fly attempted to flee. They were "discouraged" from so many failed attempts. Breaking the word down, they lost their courage, "dis-couraged".

Knowing the definitions of words and breaking them into two has helped me put many things in life back together. And, as most people know, courage is following through with what you need to do, despite the fear. I had attempted to quit so many times and every time found myself back in the jar of addiction. Finally, I found a way out, to fly and be free.

The scope of this chapter is the 12 Step program. And, the programs are based on a book, not just meetings alone. In the book's beginning, chapters hold the instructions to working the 12 Steps and the 2nd half of the book include personal stories that were written by members who have shared their experiences. I am attempting to write this chapter as if it was for the "Big Book" as we call it in the program. And, stay on topic. H.O.P.E. Hearing Other People's Experiences.

I have taken note that the ones who only attend meetings and do not read or work the 12 steps in the book, are the ones who do not succeed or often even survive. As a member you are always an example. We are both the student and the teacher at the same time. Each one of us has the opportunity to deliver a sermon to the clergy. And, sometimes, when these testimonies get off topic, you may find yourself being held hostage by someone who is trying to unscramble their heavily abused brain. I find these scenarios somewhat meditational in the sense that you are forced to stay quiet and listen. The premise of which I approach my meditations.

Either way, making sense or non-sense, you are an example. An example of what to do or of what not to do. To succeed and survive, we follow the examples of those who have an extended time period of sobriety. At the end of the day, the old timers are truly the ones who show us how to live one day at a time, clean and sober. To be or not to be, what to do or what not to do, to stay alive or die. In the meetings we hear that the "newcomer" is the most important person in the meeting. For me, the newcomers are a reminder that: It is easier to stay sober than it is to get sober.

EGO; Edging God Out. This is one of many great acronyms echoing through the rooms of A.A. and N.A. Acronyms used as tools to repair the character defects of which we are hardly even aware of. This helps us to get our feet back on the ground. Once we are no longer blinded by our ego, we can see that there is a power greater than ourselves. By continuing to go to meetings and not drinking in between meetings, we learn more about our ego, as we go. They are separate yet one in the same, but never at the same time. A battle between two mindsets. Being aware of which one I am thinking with has been very enlightening.

The little voice in an alcoholics brain (when the ego is speaking) usually says, "Have a drink, you'll feel better". This is danger and destruction calling, because in the long run, we would have felt better had we not gotten drunk. Ego and alcohol have so much in common by supporting a false awesomeness. Both make us feel that we are better looking and smarter, when they are active. But, by taking the alcohol away, we can see a little clearer without our beer goggles blurring our vision. The ego's voice is a bit more tricky though, since it shares the same sound as our speaking voice. Deciphering the differences between our spiritual thoughts and our egotistical thinking helps tremendously.

They say it's a spiritual program, not a religious program. My sponsor had taught me to forget everything that religion had taught me about God. Then come up with a concept of my own understanding based on my personal life experiences. Everything has changed for me, yet I still use the word "God" to describe how I search for help. Everyone that I've met in the program is normally unusual. The same, yet different, and our beliefs vary as well. As long as those beliefs are congruent with the understanding that we need help from a power greater than ourselves. This change in our belief system becomes highly effective. Even though our backgrounds differ, our foregrounds come together into a harmony where "me" becomes "we".

I am responsible for using words that are from my heart and truthful from my perception. It is up to others to translate what I am saying so that they can understand for themselves what they see from their point of view. The rest is out of my hands. Anyone can turn good into bad and bad into good, since perspective is subjective.

As we learn from each other in the program, both as student and teacher, some mis-information does leak through. Though if you look closely, you'll clearly see that the person who is sharing is trying to be honest. Their life depends upon it. H.O.W. "Honest, Open-mindedness, Willingness".

The ancient image of an old man on a throne judging me to an eternity of heaven or hell is not how I envision my new concept of God. The grey beard; the story about Santa Claus. Another judgmental old man, watching over you, eventually made its way to casting out rewards or punishments, pointing out good and bad. AA/NA members are not bad people trying to be good, but sick people trying to get well. Guilt is seldom helpful, though remorse can repair.

From time to time, I like to believe that I have an original thought. And, this one derived from the word "forgive". Believe in Him or not, I do believe that Jesus's message was just that - for-giveness. I personally link this to my program by the understanding that resentments kill. And here comes the original thought, centered on breaking two words down. "For-giving", which is generosity at its core. You are giving someone or something permission to carry on without your resentment.

The 2nd word is "For-getting". A more selfish act. It is because we get to (for-get). It's (for/getting) the resentment. I get to relieve myself of the burden of that memory. Therefore in my theory, it's twice as nice to forgive and forget!

Continuous sobriety requires that we are vigilantly aware of when our ego-mind is doing the thinking. Our ego is not our amigo. Our spirit-mind is much more friendly. When we are thinking with our spirit or soul-mind, we are much more at peace. The spirit/soul knows no time; it is eternal. No constraints, no timeline to cause anxiety. Being spirit-minded removes "the waiting". You can tell an alcoholic "yes" or "no", but "waiting" is almost impossible for us. We are not known for our patience. At times it's difficult to keep this in our mind, as the ego always tries to return and impatiently at that.

From my experience with anxiety, I found it to feel like a temporary hell on earth. And, the little voices in my head were narrating with a sense of urgency that this feeling would last an eternity. Simultaneously contradicting itself by telling me that I would die at any moment now!

In the rooms of recovery you may hear this, "Religion is for people who are afraid of going to hell, while spirituality is for people who have been to hell and do not want to go back". Remembering and understanding this makes me strive to consistently think soul-minded.

As I ponder upon my ancient past, it seems possible that a lot of my using was a control issue. Always trying to control how I felt my feelings. I'm a fun-addict as in a fanatic. What I used to do for fun turned into tuning out anything that was not fun. A good example would be my job cleaning swimming pools. To perform my work, I found marijuana to be as important of a chemical as chlorine. When using substances to control my circumstances, I felt better about the hand I was dealt. Of course, this cut into my profits, especially since I smoked only the most expensive pot.

Many who first attend A.A. for their drinking problem, assume that they can go on smoking pot. For me and the majority of A.A. members, we find this impossible. Any drug use always led us back to drinking eventually. In the Narcotics Anonymous literature, it states that alcohol is a drug. So, total abstinence from any mind altering substance is required for true sobriety.

I've heard many times from recovering alcoholics that "we have a disease that tells us that we don't". Denial runs deep. In my own observation I've found marijuana to claim that it is not a drug. A definition of what a drug is to me is: "Something that is extremely hard to quit". So, if you are an addict, choose your addictions wisely. I chose to be addicted to sobriety, a sober-holic.

12 Step programs are not just for addicts. Al-Anon is congruent in the way that it can bring serenity to its members. My mother is a very active Al-Anon member and I have witnessed the change in her. Through the same 12 Steps that I took, she has received a whole new healthy outlook on life. We enjoy the miracles that we have seen and received. It's become a bond that goes beyond. We even share the same slogans, as "Keep it Simple". Being

overwhelmed is never helpful. To over-explain adds confusion. "Easy does it" is a more efficient way to go about it. And, witnessing the transformation of these people is to observe a miracle.

By definition, a miracle is an event of which one cannot explain. Yet, here I am trying to explain how it works. When words are all we have, we use what we got. But, actually words are not our only tool. We lead by example, monkey see, monkey do. Once again, you can be an example of what to do or an example of what not to do. It's easy to spot the ones who "walk the walk" from the ones who only "talk the talk".

Early on in my sobriety, an old biker who was my sponsor, took me to a prison so that we could "carry the message". It was a moonless night way up a country road, which added to the dramatics of speaking to a room full of criminals. I don't remember what I said that night, but I will never forget what my sponsor, Gary, had said. His explanation of the miracle of sobriety was electrifying. Comparing it to the light switch and the light bulb. He even went over near the door and switched it on and off to intensify the dramatization.

The point being was that generally few people in the room/world can perfectly understand how the electrical currents powered the light. How I received his pseudo sermon was that an electrician was capable of explaining the logistics of it. And in my attempt to calculate his testimony, I came to the conclusion that there just might be as many "sober-holics" in the world as there are electricians. And, without former electricians to enlighten the rookie electricians, we would all be sitting in the dark, drunk!

One man whom I was sponsoring in the Philippines had overdosed and died. This reminded me that I was lucky to be alive, being that he was 44, the same age I was when I had gotten sober. I also had one sponsee who was more afraid of dying from his addiction than of his H.I.V. diagnosis. It's been said that when you join the program you should buy a blue book and a black suit. The program is in the book and if you stick around long enough, you will be attending some funerals. And, if you don't stick around, you might be showing up for your own funeral a bit early. The truth is, lies kill! And, complete honesty is a vital requirement. H.O.W. "Honesty, Willingness and Open-mindedness" once again and again . . . . Seeing so much death has made me truly thankful, as I make a conscious effort to be late for my own funeral.

Since I live on both sides of the planet from time to time, I have a sponsor in California and another in the Philippines. Dan, who has been there since before my sobriety date of 2-15-11, had helped me work the steps to the best of my ability. Fernan, in the Philippines, and I have never gone through the steps together. I had over 3 years when I'd asked him to sponsor me. Fernan is quite a humble guru to most of the members here. He has some background in counseling and has completed a lot of training in this field. His advice is always sound, as he sponsors more people than any other that I have known.

Fernan has seriously made the Philippines a much more manageable place for my life. And, when my parents came over to visit, Fernan treated us like he was our very own private tour guide. In his van, he took us to museums and some unique places that only a true local would know about. Also from time to time, his van (the meeting mobile) fills up with A.A. and N.A. members and heads out to visit beautiful beaches and glorious water-falls. And, until I acquired a motorcycle, he used to pick me up on his way to meetings. During those commutes some memorable conversations took place. His presence has a calming effect. Fernan and I experience friendship and sponsorship as we share adventures and much laughter together. Dan, on the other hand, and the other side of the world, is always there when I'm in California. My 1st few years were shaky and unstable, but he offered con-sistency as we read the Big Book together and fully worked the steps, with several meetings a week as well. He was of vital importance in helping me achieve that illusive 1st year of sobriety.

Part of Dan's directions to me were to look up the main words in all 12 Steps. To understand the true definitions of the key words would help me to reattach a firmer grip on reality. And to this day, I am grateful for his suggestions/directions and his general concern for my well-being.

Dan's journey has been very tough. His type of alcoholic almost always dies drunk. A true life or death situation. Unfortunately, he has had some life-threatening relapses. I currently have more sobriety time than him. Fortunately, as far as I know, he has remained undead by the grace of God. Dan is one of those gracious souls who can save hundreds, yet might not be able to save himself. I truly believe that he would take a bullet for another, and in a way, he has.

I consider Dan my sponsor (when in California) for a lifetime. Which one of our lifetimes has yet to be revealed? Dan, I consider to be a true friend as well. We have also had adventures surfing and skating, flowing and growing. This friendship business may sound far-fetched, nevertheless skeptical as I was, living it is knowing it.

A home group is usually the meeting that you regularly attend. There your local recognition is found, where familiar faces are seen. A "God Shot" this may be, in the U.S. my home group is named "The Staying Alive" group. And in the Philippines, my home group is pronounced "Buhay Ka Pa", which translates into (staying alive). Coincidence? There are no coincidences! Only simplicity synchronized with serendipity, fused congruently with consciousness.

The program has not changed, but the Steps do appear differently to me now that I have changed. Subjectivity is in perpetual change. "We do not see the world as it is, we see it as we are". This program has reformed my mindset to a newly formed reality. "It works, if you work it". And, truthfully there is some work that needs to be done to allow us to be honest with ourselves. Sometimes requiring a pen and paper, we find writing to be very therapeutic. We follow guidelines and take direction. We work on killing our ego, before it kills us. That little (sometimes big) voice in our head proves to be the problem centered in between our ears. We need to learn how to take responsibility for our own action. Blaming is not an option.

To become enlightened, first we need to become aware. When problems with people, places and things arise, we ask ourselves these 4 questions to assume accountability and keep our side of the street clean. These key questions unlock our serenity when answered honestly. Where am I actively (1) Self-centered (2) Resentful (3) Dishonest (4) Fearful.

We take an inventory of the things that only we have control of, before they have control of our thoughts. Resentments are deadly to an addict/alcoholic. Normal people or (Normies), as they are often referred to, have the luxury of holding grudges. They may get uncomfortable and even miserable, but most likely it will not pull the trigger to drink for them. When we are in the wrong, we need to admit it and do so promptly. This clears our mind and aids in our survival.

I could go on and on about recovery, because it's an ongoing program always going on. If you are interested, alcoholic or not, we welcome you to sit in on A.A. and N.A. meetings, and now even online with Zoom meetings. Most of the people, most of the time, are very friendly and their stories are wondrous. I've found some meetings to be more entertaining than a Cinema show; it's the best show on earth because it is full of wild characters. Though most attendees are not there for the entertainment, they are there as a matter of life or death. The emotions vary with extreme depth. One moment someone may be crying and a few minutes later the whole room is laughing until their bellies hurt. Tears of love, laughter, joy and sorrow are all shed. It's not always a laughing matter or laughing like the Mad Hatter. Either way, that does remind me of a joke about cocaine that I once heard in a meeting. "I never really liked coke, I just loved the way it smelled".

We deal with what we've been dealt, by sharing what we have felt. Lifelong friendships develop as a result of trying to make our life last longer. And, together we become stronger. More will be revealed as the onion is peeled.

I almost forgot to mention these important words and their definitions. Reasonable; Sane. Unreasonable; insane. These words helped me to unravel a revelation. I felt legitimately sane, again!

A few years into my sobriety while at a doctor's appointment, I asked the doctor if she had noticed anything different about me now that I've had over 3 years without drugs and alcohol. She looked at me and replied, "Well, you seem much more 'reasonable' now." I felt legitimately sane, at last!

CHAPTER 12

ILLUSIONS ABOUT CONCLUSIONS

"Fear has the ability to cause more damage than the danger ever could"

Not until any situation is thoroughly thought through can this premise be completely understood. "Most solutions create new and different problems". A true solution does not involve tradeoffs. This was not taken into consideration throughout the whole COVID hysteria.

Looking forward to getting us away from this pure madness. On March 22, 2020, my wife and I left our home just after sunrise and headed to the airport with flight tickets from the Philippines to the U.S.A. Shortly after our ride had dropped us off, we discovered that our flight had been cancelled and that any future flights would be up in the air (pun intended), as our sense of humor was all that we had left. The Coronaflu protocols left the world's populations with very little levity. Protocols that were put in place indefinitely, based on overhyped predictions.

We found ourselves deep in the middle of an angry mob. Hundreds of panicking travelers were bumping elbows and spitting out yells of frustration toward a confused staff of employees, that were following the protocols of the new normal. After that ordeal, over the next 3 months we had 5 more booked flights to the U.S.A. and 4 more flights cancelled. Finally, I caught a flight, but unfortunately, without my wife.

My wife, Yolly, has owned an apartment building long before we met. At this point after 3 months of not allowing people to work, the government's decision to embrace lockdowns caused many people to become homeless.

They had no money to pay rent. So, she decided to stay behind to manage the catastrophe of her tenants having to vacate their homes.

Leaving the airport without her was in no doubt the saddest time in our marriage. Not knowing when we would be permitted to see each other again was heartbreaking! To find some strength by looking for a positive, I found out that I positively love her and I also was positive that missing her would be painful.

A brave and comprehensive book named "The Price of Panic" might have saved the world if it had been read by all. It was one of the first to be published within the first year of the madness. Many of the books to follow seem to come up with the same conclusion that "the forced lockdowns were mankind's biggest blunder in history".

Before I had left the Philippines, I lined up a job resuming my lifelong profession of cleaning swimming pools. A beautiful small town named Ojai is where I found myself poolside once again. My father had offered to provide me with a camping trailer to live in, if I could find a place to stage it. The next month, after landing in the "land of the brave and home of the free", I had found a spot on the other side of the world where the madness was much more mild.

A Godsend really. A land owner of one of the pools that I was servicing had full-hookups and rented the spot to me for a very nice price. As if God was taking custom orders from me, He put a world class skateboard park a few miles from my long-term camping spot. Thank God, the One who works in mysterious ways.

I have lots of respect and compassion for the people who were forced to wear masks while working. Every day I was grateful that I was not forced to wear one. The Filipinos were forced to wear masks and shields for longer than most of the world was forced to wear masks. It's been six months into the fourth year and the majority of the Filipinos still wear masks voluntarily, but mandated at most places of employment. From my observations, it is out of force of habit (a psychosis). It is sad to see all those beautiful smiles covered up.

It may sound weird, but I believe that we live in a make believe world, where whatever we are made to believe, we are compelled to comply. These forced beliefs end up causing resentment once we realize that it is a false truth, an inter-subjective reality. Our mind is not always our own. Our sense of truth and perception were constantly being manipulated by the media, more so during this time than any other. A lie told a thousand times becomes a truth; a consensual hallucination.

Over the next fourteen months, I would live, work, surf, skate and spend every Monday with Mom in the States. Ten months being without my wife was the hard part. She finally made it to California and stayed with me for 3 months before we returned to the Philippines together.

At this point worldwide traveling came with excessive red tape, including restrictions, COVID insurance, permits and certificates on top of already existing visas and passports. We had to be vaccinated to fly. Ultimately the vaccines did not prevent people from contracting COVID-19. Ten-day isolation facilities were required upon landing in the Philippines and contact tracing was mandatory.

Hotels were transformed into isolation facilities. From anywhere between $60 to $120 a night, you could arrange to be monitored. I really missed feeling the sun on my skin during those 10 days.

On the 7th day we paid $70 each for a swab test, then waited three more days for the results. I asked the nurse what would happen to us if we received a false positive? She replied, "Then our government will decide what happens to you". Talk about stressful!!

A year later my wife and I tried to return to the U.S.A. But, I received a false positive COVID test and the authorities insisted that I was "asymptomatic". So, back to isolation. About 2 weeks later and hundreds of dollars in expenses, we were able to fly. The whole 2 weeks I felt physically perfect, but mentally sick. By that point the protocols had driven me insane. The explanation that most seemed to accept was: "One of the symptoms is that you have no symptoms".

I love this quote from Mark Twain: "It's easier to fool people than to convince them that they have been fooled". Our egos may be responsible for that type of blindness. In a "make believe" reality, the media controls the majority with what they can "make" them "believe". This misinformation creates a false truth and to disagree can label you as crazy. In some places, they have made activism as illegal as terrorism. Fear seems unescapable, either some are afraid of COVID or others are afraid to speak out against this flu-pandemic or flu-pandemonium. Depending on your experience, you saw it as one or the other.

In several of the books about awakening, they mention that there will be a very dark time preceding the age of enlightenment. A time so ridiculously stupid that you would have to have zero ability to think for yourself, to not recognize the absurdities. Hence the saying, "It must get worse before it gets better". I have found this to be an essential part of recovery.

We are living through a twilight zone dimension. Two iconic books were written about 70 years ago, "Brave New World" and "1984". They were science fiction at the time, but nowadays they resemble history books. They look like predictions of states of surveillance and insanity. And, George Orwell in "1984" puts it very accurately when he said "Orthodoxy is unconsciousness". These dystopian novels may have been very useful, had we used them as warning signs. We could have used the hindsight in 2020; hindsight is 20/20.

There are many very talented Filipino skateboarders living in the Philippines. Even though at times they are without tennis shoes, that doesn't stop them. After lockdowns lightened up a little, many skateboarders were left without boards. I've seen many doing kick-flips in flip-flops. So, I started a non-profit organism/fun-dation as I like to call it. "Boarders without Boards" has provided many kids with skateboards and shoes. All the money was sent to me from generous friends from California who became donators to the skaters. The kids and I are extremely appreciative that they shared some of their stimulus package to replenish the much needed shoes and boards.

I have never had a child of my own, but now I am having a fatherly feeling from what I am experiencing with "Boarders without Boards". Occasionally I would even skate the streets with them. The kids age between 12 and 17, the stage when drugs and alcohol can seem very inviting. So I try to carry the message about sobriety and share some positivity as a mentor figure. A couple of their parents thanked me for the moral support that came along with the shoes plus boards. I believe that we have made some lasting friendships, which has always been a big part of skateboarding.

There will always be some confusions when dealing with the illusions about conclusions. I thought I knew when I was retiring from my occupation in 2007 as a swimming pool tech, but it turned out to be unknown. Then it happened 4 more times, allowing me to re-retire 3 times. Done and begun, recycling themselves again and again. "It never stops starting" is only true for so long. Eventually the body has the final word. Up until the age of 55, my body still allowed me to drop into an empty swimming pool on a skateboard and clean a full one with sparkling water. Then the knees and hip began to scream a pain which deafened any sounds of enjoyment that I could find by continuing either activity.

Now I fill my days in other ways during what I believe to be my final retirement. When one retires, forgetting what day of the week it is becomes easy. Currently the scheduled A.A. meetings help keep the week in perspective.

We can't have bad without good and vice versa. The lockdowns gave birth to zoom meetings. This has allowed me to attend my "Staying Alive" A. A. group meeting in California from all the way over here in the Philippines. On the other side of the coin, we lost our facility where the "Buhay Ka Pa" group gathered here in the Philippines. Due to the lockdowns and the unemployment that it caused, our local facility became an indefinite place of residency for many of the displaced Filipinos that had been affected.

A.A. meetings are important. Alcoholism can just as easily be called a pandemic. Personally in the last two years (2020-2022), I have known more people that have drunk themselves to death than have died from COVID complications. Which reminds me, when feeling like I was at death's door with a hangover, I would refer to it as having a case of the Bottle-Flu.

I found a perfect location to start up a new meeting right across the street from my home. Most of the meetings here in Manila are spoken using Tagalog. I do my best to understand without always being able to do so. And, since I was going to be in charge of getting this new meeting started, I structured it to be an English speaking A.A. meeting. So far the meeting has been successful and continues to grow in its attendance, though its future is unknown.

The "Normally Unusual" group A.A. meeting meets every Tuesday. I chose to use this name for 2 reasons. First of course, after the name of this book. Secondly, because "Normally Unusual" perfectly describes each one of the A.A. members, worldwide actually. We are all uniquely the same, while experiencing perpetual personal change together.

Another illusion about a conclusion, was believing that the remainder of my days would be lived out as a single man. And then, this happened

It was a Thanksgiving Day celebration in 2013 at my parent's house and my brother, Scott, invited his girlfriend, Girlie, and her parents to join us for dinner that night. I found these people to be interesting, being of Filipino descent and very decent people. I have always found finding differences to be more interesting than similarities. As I spoke with who would eventually become my brother's father-in-law (Scott married Girlie), he told me about a much younger cousin of his that was the same age as me.

Not wanting to believe that the remainder of my days would be that of a single man, I requested (Mario) "Kuya Mar" to call up his cousin right there and then on the spot. The 16-hour time difference between the U.S. and the Philippines fell on an hour in her morning where she was available to talk to this eager American. I took the phone into another room for some privacy and we spoke for over 30 minutes. By the end of the call, I had already fallen in love with her voice. So far so good!

Soon after that, Yolly and I scheduled daily conversations at her 9 a.m., my 5 p.m. I would buy calling cards, for at this point in my life, I still had not participated in Facebook or video calls. We exchanged a few still photos through email, but it would not be until April, 2014 when she flew over to California that we could see each other's smiles in motion.

Around this same time, a reality T.V. show had come on the air named "90 day Fiancé"! Well, our encounter was somewhat similar to that, but much more rapid! Yolanda landed in California looking as beautiful as any potential wife that I could have personally asked God for to spend the remaining of my days with. In less than 2 weeks, I put a ring on that pretty little thing and on May 10, 2014, we were married!

Love moves mountains, even across oceans. A new space, a new place and even living amongst a new race. Life would change and I along with it. I knew some things would be more difficult and some less difficult. I chose to live in her world with her, rather than mine without her. Neither one of us would be the same after the love of my life took my name.

My new stepson, Michael, picked us up from the airport in Manila. Primed with jetlag, we drove to their house. It is attached to the 12-unit apartment building which Yolly owns. It is located on the same street as the house where she was born in 1967. I'm still impressed that she wasn't born in a hospital. And, even more impressed that she now has become a landlord to many, just down the street from the house where her mother gave birth to her from inside.

Once it registered just how far and different from California the Philippines is, I was overwhelmed; my next step was to work through the cultural shock and the emotions that go hand in hand with every major life changing experience. Every time we held hands, I felt a grip of reassurance.

I knew she was going to be a wonderful wife and that has proven to be true. The only job that I have now is to be wonderful husband. In the Philippines there would be zero opportunity for employment for me that could compare to my career back in America. This brought on a normally unusual early retirement, which provided me with the opportunity to write the book, "Normally Unusual".

Had I met the love of my life much earlier, odds are that it might not have lasted. Sobriety is a major factor in making this loving life with Yolly possible. The principles learned from the 12-Step recovery program are tools that I utilize to keep this marriage in tune. The life that we share now really wouldn't be conducive to the party lifestyle of my past. One really needs to be present to enjoy the gift of marriage.

The conundrum is that the less time we have available (lifespan) to live this connected life together, the more time I want to live it to postpone the ultimate good-bye. "Less is more" is a relatively famous saying that can be applied to many situations. With Yolly, the "less" time that we have to be alive together, the "more" I realize how much I love her. Now that I've got what I've always wanted, more time is wanted to enjoy the togetherness. I was dying to fall in love, now I'm dying to stay alive.

Deep thoughts, I have them more than some and less than others, but I have never considered myself common. A common question for mankind might be: Is all random or reason? I believe that there is a reason for all the randomness. The sane, the insane. Reasonable and the unreasonable. The order and the chaos. What's understood and what's misunderstood. Throughout life and the infinity of death.

Drawing a conclusion helps us to believe in reason, like a crutch.

Non-conclusive thought leaves room for doubt. This is where faith is required. With faith, the calculation is complete without the aid of a conclusion. Some believe that if it cannot be measured, then it cannot exist. This type of scientific mindset could make it difficult to believe in something that you cannot fully understand, immeasurable. The human mind by design is not capable of the comprehension of afterlife. If it was, then there would be no need for faith.

I can't prove or even explain sufficiently these conceptual theories, I only entertain their possibilities. The only thing that I am completely convinced by experience is that: Yesterday was different and tomorrow will be the same, through the imagination of today. And, that unusual feeling is normal.

AFTER WORDS

"NORMALLY UNUSUAL"

"Life seems to be unusual . . . . normally" ~ VK

Thank you so much for entertaining my story. This has been a mind expanding experience to write, to live. I hope it expanded your horizons from both sides of this hemisphere. To see further was also my focus, to envision the unseen. Reliving my life through a constructed memory, I have found this to be a form of reincarnation. And as a bonus, now even if we have never met, we have interacted indirectly, yet somewhat effectively.

It has been difficult to write this story, to put all of my scattered thoughts into order. As hard as it is to believe, writing it was possibly as hard as it was to live. Writing takes perseverance to tell a story without making a single sound. Never stop starting and forget that an end is inevitable nevertheless.

In my early adult years, my imagination came up with a concept, a theory that purgatory was a room in-between life and the after-life. In this room there would be a T.V. replaying a video of my life. It would take me equal time to watch as my life took to live. Throughout   this duration, the illusion of time would be void, in comparison to how we currently measure its construct. This purgatory would be a spec in comparison to eternity. Then at the end of the show, my life in review, I would decide if I was going to heaven or hell. No one is harder on myself than me, so I thought that this would be a fair critic. But, now after writing this book and reviewing my life, I have come to somewhat of a conclusion that this may be an illusion.

As for what's next, God only knows. And, if you know God, then you have some ideas also. Something led up to our being here, something unknown, as it will be after. Pondering a mystery full of great unknown, with a full tank of faith and hope seems like the best way to travel through this journey. I have a feeling that it will lead us beyond any explanation or expectation that words could have the ability to provide. The paradox is that there may come a time when we are conscious outside of the constructs of time. This life is linear here on earth, such is the way of words. Thoughts are ideas constructed from words. So it makes sense to me that what may come after, goes beyond thought, beyond words. After Words!

(LAST WORD)

P.S. Writing a book is by far no easy task. Though, if your circumstances allow you time, I highly recommend facing this extremely rewarding challenge, even if it never gets published.

As I was having my doubts that this book would ever see the light, nevertheless, I attempted to write the remembrances of my life chronologically, the best I could.

Life flows linear, as well as the trail. As do the lines in this book. Though, memories do not. Every day they yearn not to fade away . . . .

www.ingramcontent.com/pod-product-compliance
Lightning Source LLC
Chambersburg PA
CBHW051516120626
46551CB00012B/950